SHERLEY'S CAT BOOK

The Complete Book of Cat Care

D1434063

Written by a
Veterinary Surgeon

Illustrated by
Judy Friedlander
and Gillian Croucher

SHERLEY'S DIVISION
ASHE LABORATORIES LTD

Contents

23rd Edition 1986
© 1984 Ashe Laboratories Ltd, Kingston Road, Leatherhead, Surrey, U.K.
Printed in England by *Kingsdale Press PLC,* Reading, Berks.

Chapter 1

CHOOSING AND KNOWING YOUR CAT

Cats have been established as household pets and friends of man for many thousands of years. They were revered by the ancient Egyptians and their ceremonially mummified remains have been found with those of their owners in the pyramids. However, if the *Just So* stories of Kipling are to be believed, the cat was the last of the animals to accept domestication in exchange for the warmth of the camp fire and to this day most cats retain a certain aloofness in their affection for their owners, rather than the unquestioning devotion of dogs.

It was probably the Romans who first introduced the cat to Britain, although there was and still is, a native wild cat in Scotland which has never been domesticated. In the middle ages the enthusiasm for cats rather declined and probably few were kept as pets, but they were valued for their ability to catch rats and mice and a manuscript of that time quotes the current price for a mousing cat at somewhere between a farthing and a halfpenny.

The popular pet

However today cats seem to be at a peak of popularity in the civilized world. It seems that no calendar, poster, or advertisement is complete unless a cat is included somewhere. They can be used to promote almost anything. It may be an elegant Siamese, a fluffy Persian kitten, or just an ordinary everyday cross-bred cat but there is somehow a charm in the totally characteristic attitudes and behaviour, a cattiness in the nicest sense of the word, that makes cat lovers everywhere stop and smile and look again.

Shows

While it is probably true to say that cat shows are more fun for owners than for cats, competitive shows (run under the auspices of the National Cat Club and the Governing Council of the Cat Fancy) have done much to popularise cats as pets and to encourage a proper sense of concern for their welfare. These shows were first started towards the end of the last century and both Queen Victoria and Edward VII were known to attend.

3

At that time prizes were awarded for the fattest and heaviest cats but today we have a more rational appreciation of show points and most owners realise that cats should be sleek and healthy but not overweight.

Cat plusses

Today's changing circumstances, when in many households people are out at work all day, make the cat especially suitable as a family pet. They do not need exercising when you come home tired at night. They are ideal for busy people (or lazy people), or for the elderly who love to have a pet, but can no longer manage the long walks which a dog needs. They can be left alone in the house through the day without unkindness: after all they sometimes sleep for 12 hours at a time if it suits them whether their owners are in or not. They do not bark or create a disturbance to annoy neighbours and in these days when pets in towns are getting so much adverse publicity it is worth remembering that cats do not foul footpaths (although it is true that they do sometimes dig up flower beds).

Costs

Feeding costs are low, or at least they should be. It is true that some owners spend large sums on costly delicacies for their cats but this is more for their own pleasure and satisfaction than from any real need to do so. A healthy cat which has been sensibly reared will keep fit and contented on the good quality tinned foods that are available today. Faddy cats are as a rule those which have been overfed.

One or two?

Having made the point that one cat in the home is a good thing, why not consider having two? There is no doubt that in most cases a cat's life is more enjoyable if there is another cat in the house and their games and scraps and the interplay of relationships between the two provide endless amusement and entertainment for their owners.

However while feeding costs should not be high it is important to remember before embarking on too large a family that veterinary costs today may be a considerable item and accidents and illnesses occur when they are least expected; health-wise two cats definitely cost more than one. There are now some insurance schemes for pets which can prove very useful if a major illness occurs or an operation is needed but it must be stressed that this will not pay for routine treatments such as vaccination or neutering.

Insurance

The various animal welfare organisations (RSPCA, PDSA, Blue Cross, etc) have branches in nearly all areas today and do great work in caring for the pets of people who are unable to afford to visit a private veterinary surgeon. A cat should never be allowed to suffer because of financial problems. The yellow pages of the telephone directory will almost certainly give the address of some organisation which is willing to help in genuine cases of need.

Although cats are remarkably trouble free pets, the care of any living thing involves some responsibility.

Proper care

It is not necessary to buy a licence for a cat (which is perhaps a pity) and indeed cats hardly exist at all in the eyes of the law, except in relation to the rabies regulations and in the sense that they are protected by the Prevention of Cruelty to Animals Act. It is only too easy to acquire a cat and then abandon it if it becomes a nuisance. This seems to happen most of all at holiday times but real animal lovers would not go away without first making sure that their pet was left in good hands.

SKELETON OF THE CAT
(and ordinary descriptions of the bones)

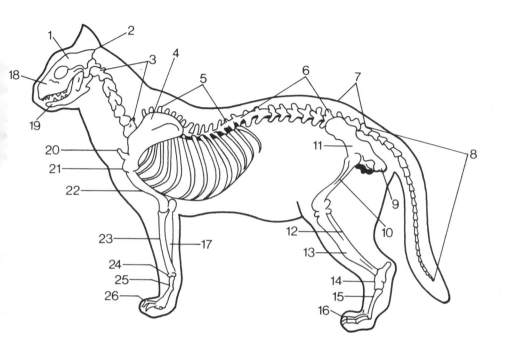

(1) Cranium (Top of Skull)
(2) Occiput (Back of Skull)
(3) Cervical Vertebrae (Neck)
(4) Scapula (Shoulder Blade)
(5) Dorsal Vertebrae (Top Back)
(6) Lumbar Vertebrae (Back)
(7) Sacrum Vertebrae (Hindquarters)
(8) Coccygeal Vertebrae (Tail)
(9) Pubis (Lower Pelvis)
(10) Femur (Thigh)
(11) Pelvis (Hindquarters)
(12) Fibula (Thinner Rear Leg Bone)
(13) Tibia (Thicker Rear Leg Bone)

(14) Tarsus (Rear Ankle)
(15) Metatarsus (Rear Foot)
(16) Rear Phalanges (Toes)
(17) Ulna (Rear Forearm Bone)
(18) Nasal Bone
(19) Mandible (Lower Jaw)
(20) Sternum (Breast Bone)
(21) Ribs
(22) Humerus (Upper Arm—Foreleg)
(23) Radius (Front Forearm Bone)
(24) Carpus (Wrist—Front Ankle)
(25) Metacarpus (Paw—Front Foot)
(26) Front Phalanges (Toes)

There is a population explosion in the cat (as well as the human) world at present, which means that neutering really is important if we are to ensure that the numbers of cats are to be limited to those for which caring homes can be found. It is sad that even in the Western world where we consider that we care for the welfare of animals each town has its colony of homeless and unwanted strays.

It has been estimated that a bitch could produce 4,400 offspring in a period of 7 years. Female cats breed even more frequently so the possible number of descendants of an un-neutered queen in her own life time is staggering (and of course the males must take some of the credit or blame for the number as well).

A great deal is written at the present time about the diseases which man can catch from animals. While the common internal parasites of the cat do not normally affect man, cases of disease in children and in kennel workers have been reported as a result of accidental infection with visceral larval migrans (the intermediate stage in the life cycle of the roundworm—see Chapter 5). While this condition is rare, it is very serious and it must be stressed that it is important to see that pets are kept free from parasites and that a high standard of hygiene is maintained.

Ringworm (a fungal skin disease) can be caught from cats and some unfortunate people are allergic to animal hair which rules out pet keeping altogether. Cat fleas do bite people sometimes but they much prefer the taste of their natural host and only constitute an occasional nuisance. In other words while the views of those who feel that animals should be banned from the home altogether cannot be totally disregarded, the risk to man is very small and most people would agree that it is far outweighed by the psychological benefit.

There is today an absolute abundance of different breeds of cat to choose from, although probably the Siamese and the Persian remain top favourites. Each has its own particular attraction and breeding or showing pedigree cats can provide a very interesting hobby. However praising pure bred cats should not make us overlook the ordinary English cross-breds. They come in a huge variety of coat, colour and length and each one has its own particular charm.

Cats today, just like people, are living longer as a result of better feeding and better care and through the introduction of antibiotics and other modern drugs which help to combat the diseases which used to shorten their lives. The record for longevity today is held by a cat which lived to be 28 but many household pets reach the age of 16 or 17. In other words the small financial outlay in buying and caring for a cat should be well repaid. If you look after your cat well he should be with you for a long time to come.

VARIETIES OF CATS

Cats are divided into two main classes: long-hairs and short-hairs, the short-haired group being subdivided into British and Foreign. The latter group includes not only the Siamese, Burmese and Abyssinian but also the Rex (curly coated) cats. A brief description of the varieties of cats recognised by the Governing Council of the Cat Fancy is given below but anyone who is interested in the more technical details of show points and faults in the various breeds should write to: The Secretary, Dovefields, Petworth Road, Witley, Surrey GU8 5QW, for the current booklet of the 'Standards of Points' enclosing a cheque or postal order for £1.50 and a stamped addressed envelope.

LONG-HAIRED

These are the so-called Persian cats which have the typical long flowing coat on body and tail, a rather cobby appearance to the body and a round head with a short nose and large wide open, round eyes.

	Coat	*Eyes*
Black Variety 1	Lustrous raven black—no white hairs or markings	Round copper or deep orange with no green rim
Blue-Eyed White Variety 2	Pure white, without mark or shade of any kind	Large round and deep blue
Orange-Eyed White Variety 2a	Pure white, without mark or shade of any kind	Orange or copper
Odd-Eyed White Variety 2b	Pure white, without mark or shade of any kind	One eye deep blue and one eye orange or copper
Blue Variety 3	Any shade of blue allowable, no markings, shadings or any white hairs	Deep orange or copper, large and round without a trace of green
Red-Self Variety 4	Deep rich red, without markings	Large round and deep copper
Cream Variety 5	Pure and sound throughout without shading or markings, pale to medium	Large, round and deep copper
Smoke Variety 6 Blue Smoke Variety 6a	*Colour*—Body: black shading to silver on the sides and flanks. Mask and feet: black with no markings. Frill and ear tufts: silver. Under-colour: as nearly white as possible	Orange or copper in colour, large and round
Blue Smoke	*Colour*—Body: blue shading to silver on the sides and flanks. Mask and feet: blue with no markings. Frill and ear tufts: silver. Under-colour: as nearly white as possible	Orange or copper in colour, large and round

	Coat	Eyes
Silver Tabby Variety 7	*Colour*—Ground colour pure pale silver, with decided jet black markings; no brown tinge	Green or hazel
Brown Tabby Variety 8	*Colour and Markings* Rich tawny sable, with delicate black pencillings running down face. The cheeks crossed with two or three distinct swirls, the chest crossed by two unbroken narrow lines, butterfly markings on shoulders. Front of legs striped regularly from toes upwards. The saddle and sides to have deep bands running down and the tail to be regularly ringed	Large and round, hazel or copper
Red Tabby Variety 9	*Colour and Markings* Deep rich red colour, markings to be clearly and boldly defined, continuing on down the chest, legs and tail	Large and round, deep copper
Chinchilla Variety 10	*Colour*—The undercoat pure white, the coat on back, flanks, head, ears and tail being tipped with black; this tipping to be evenly distributed, chin, ear tufts, stomach and chest must be pure white. The tip of the nose brick-red and the visible skin on eyelids and the pads black or dark brown	Large, round emerald or blue-green
Tortoiseshell Variety 11	*Colour*—Three colours, black, red and cream, well broken into patches; colours to be bright and rich and well broken on face	Large and round, deep orange or copper
Tortoiseshell and White Variety 12	*Colour*—Three colours, black, red and cream, or their dilutions to be well distributed and broken and interspersed with white	Large and round, deep orange or copper

	Coat	Eyes
Bi-Colour Variety 12a	*Colours and Distribution*—Any solid colour and white, the patches of colour to be clear, even and well distributed. Not more than two thirds of the cat's coat to be coloured and not more than a half to be white. Face to be patched with colour and white	Large and round, deep orange or copper
Blue-Cream Variety 13	*Colour and Markings* To consist of blue and cream, softly intermingled; pastel shades	Deep copper or orange
Colourpoint Variety 13b	*Colour* 1 Seal points with cream body colour. 2 Blue points with glacial white body colour. 3 Chocolate points with ivory body colour. 4 Lilac points with magnolia body colour. 5 Red points with off white body colour. 6 Tortie points with cream body colour. 7 Cream 8 Blue cream 9 Chocolate cream 10 Lilac cream	Large, round, bright and blue
Birman Variety 13c	*Colour and Condition* The colouring is the same as Siamese, Seal and Blue but face (mask) tail and paws are dark brown in the Seals and blue/grey in the Blues. See Siamese	Bright china blue
Turkish Variety 13d	Chalk white with no trace of yellow. Auburn markings on face with white blaze. Ears white	Round, colour light amber, rims pink-skinned

BRITISH SHORT-HAIRS

These have a coat which is dense and short. They are compact cats with short legs and a tail which is thick at the base and rounded at the tip. They have a rather round head with small ears. The nose is short and straight and the eyes are large, round and wide open.

	Coat	Eyes
White Blue-Eyed Variety 14	Pure white, untinged with yellow	Very deep sapphire blue. No green rims or flecks
White Orange-Eyed Variety 14a	Pure white, untinged with yellow	Gold, orange or copper. No green rims or flecks
White Odd-Eyed Variety 14b	Pure white, untinged with yellow	One gold, orange or copper. One blue. No green rims or flecks
Black Variety 15	Jet black to roots, no rusty tinge. No white hairs anywhere	Deep copper or orange with no trace of green
Blue Variety 16	Light to medium blue, no tabby markings or white anywhere	Copper or orange
Cream Variety 17	Lighter shades preferred. Level in colour and free from markings. No sign of white anywhere	Copper or orange

CLASSIC TABBY PATTERN

The Governing Council of the Cat Fancy recommends that all markings be clearly defined and dense. Legs barred evenly with bracelets going down from the body markings to the toes. Ground colour and markings should be equally balanced. Evenly ringed tail. On the neck and upper chest there should be unbroken necklaces. On the forehead there should be a letter 'M' made by frown marks. There should be an unbroken line running back from the outer corner of the eye and there should be pencillings on the cheeks. There should be a vertical line with runs over the back of the head and extends to the shoulder markings, which should be shaped like a butterfly. Both the upper and the lower wings should be defined clearly in outline with dots inside this outline.

Cheeks

On the back there should be a line running down the spine from the butterfly to the tail and there should be a stripe on each side of this running parallel to it. These strips should be separated from each other by stripes of the ground colour. On each flank there should be a large solid oyster or blotch which should be surrounded by one or more unbroken rings. The markings on each side should be identical. All Tabby cats should be spotted in the abdominal region and the tails should be evenly ringed.

Flank

	Coat	Eyes
Silver Tabby Variety 18	Clear silver ground colour. Markings dense black	Green or hazel
Red Tabby Variety 19	Red ground colour and markings of deep rich red	Brilliant copper
Brown Tabby Variety 20	Brilliant coppery brown ground colour with dense black markings	Orange, hazel or deep yellow

MACKEREL TABBY

Head, legs and tail as for Classic Tabby. A narrow unbroken line running from the back of the head to the base of the tail. Rest of the body to be covered with narrow lines running vertically down from the spine line and to be unbroken.

	Coat	Eyes
Spotted Variety 30	Silver with black spots. Brown with black spots. Red with deep rich red spots.	Silver spotted, green or hazel. Brown spotted, orange, hazel or deep yellow. Red spotted, brilliant copper
Tortoiseshell Variety 21	Black with brilliant patches of cream and red. A red or cream blaze on the head is desirable	Brilliant copper or orange
Tortoiseshell and White Variety 22	Black, cream and red on white, equally balanced. With blaze desirable	Copper or orange
Blue Cream Variety 28	Blue and cream to be softly intermingled. No blaze	Copper or orange
Bi-Colour Variety 31	Any accepted colour and white. Not more than two thirds of the cat's coat to be coloured. White blaze desirable	Brilliant copper or orange
Smokes Variety 36	Black or blue. Undercoat pale silver	Yellow or orange

MANX VARIETY 25

In appearance the Manx cat is similar to the British Short-Hair but is of course tailless. It is a compact solid cat, with the hind legs set rather higher than the fore. Colour and eye colour correspond to the standard for the British.

FOREIGN SHORT-HAIRS

Russian Blue—This is a rather long and graceful cat, with a wedge shaped skull. The coat is a clear even blue throughout. The eyes are almond shape and vivid green, set wide apart.

Abyssinian—Again a rather fine built cat with a wedge shaped skull, with ears set well apart. The eyes are oriental shaped with a slight slant (no squint) and amber, hazel, or green and the coat is 'ticked' or 'banded' with double colour.

	Coat	*Eyes*
Usual Variety 23	Rich golden brown, ticked with black	All three varieties, amber, hazel or green
Red Variety 23a	Lustrous copper-red, ticked with chocolate	
Blue Variety 23c	Blue-grey, ticked with deeper steel blue	

Burmese—Another elegant and graceful foreign type, with slender legs and a muscular appearance. The eyes are wide set with a slight oriental slant.

Eye colour—any shade of yellow from chartreuse to amber, with golden yellow preferred. Green eyes are a serious fault in Brown Burmese, but Blue Burmese may show a slight fading of colour.

	Coat
Brown Variety 27	Rich warm seal brown with slightly darker ears and mask
Blue Variety 27a	Soft silver grey only very slightly darker on the back and tail
Chocolate Variety 27b	Warm milk chocolate with slightly darker ears and mask
Lilac Variety 27c	Pale, delicate dove-grey
Red Variety 27d	Light tangerine. Ears should be distinctly darker than the back
Brown Tortie Variety 27e	A mixture of brown and red without any obvious barring
Cream Variety 27f	Rich cream. Slight tabby markings may be found on the face
Blue Tortie Variety 27g	A mixture of blue and cream without any obvious barring
Chocolate Tortie Variety 27h	A mixture of chocolate and red without any obvious barring
Lilac Tortie Variety 27j	A mixture of lilac and cream without any obvious barring

Havana Cats Variety 29—Fine boned cats of a Siamese type, but with a rich brown coat and green oriental type eyes.

Foreign Lilac Variety 29c—Similar in appearance to the Havana but coat grey, with a pinkish tinge.

Foreign White Variety 35—Siamese in type but with pure white coat and brilliant blue eyes.

Cornish Rex Variety 33	These are cats with an unusual curly coat—including crinkled eyebrows and whiskers.
Devon Rex Variety 33a	All coat colours acceptable. The eyes are oval and colours should be in keeping with coat colour.

Korat Cats Variety 34—A more muscular or cobby variety. This variety does not carry challenge certificate status. Eyes should be large and particularly prominent. Eye aperture, which appears as well-rounded, fully open, has Asian slant when closed or partially closed; brilliant green, but amber cast acceptable. Silver-blue all over, tipped with silver and hair is short to medium in length.

Siamese—The many varieties of Siamese cats are probably the most popular of the foreign cats. They are graceful with rather slim hind legs and a long tapering tail. The eyes are oriental in shape slanting towards the nose and in various shades of blue.

	Coat	*Eyes*
Siamese (seal-pointed) Variety 24	Cream, shading gradually into pale warm fawn on the back	Clear, brilliant deep blue
Siamese (blue-pointed) Variety 24a	Body colour: glacial white. Points blue	Clear, bright, vivid blue
Siamese (chocolate-pointed) Variety 24b	Ivory colour all over. Points milk chocolate	Clear, bright, vivid blue
Siamese (lilac-pointed) Variety 24c	Off white (magnolia). Points pinkish-grey	Clear, light vivid blue (but not pale)
Siamese (tabby-pointed) Variety 32	Pale coat, preferably free from body markings. Same colour essential, but varied tones of same colour acceptable, ie, seal, blue, chocolate, lilac, red or cream	Brilliant clear blue
Tortie/Tabby Points	Similar to variety 32 but patched with red and/or cream over tabby pattern	
Siamese (Red-pointed) Variety 32a	White, shading (if any) to apricot on the back. Ears and tail bright reddish-gold	Bright vivid blue

13

	Coat	Eyes
Siamese (Tortie-pointed) Variety 32b	Restricted to points as in all Siamese: basic colour seal, blue, chocolate or lilac as in Breeds 24, 24a, 24b, 24c	Blue, as in equivalent solid colour Siamese
Cream Point Siamese Provisional Breed Variety 32c	Provisional Standard of Points as for Seal point Siamese. White shading (if any) to palest cream	Bright vivid blue

Chapter 2

WHEN YOUR CAT HAS KITTENS

Cats usually make good mothers and seem to enjoy maternity. Supervising the rearing of a litter of kittens contributes a lot of pleasure to most households, especially where there are children, who really love to watch the progress of the new arrivals. It is especially pleasant if circumstances allow, to keep at least one kitten as an addition to the family, since it provides companionship for the mother and is always valued and spoiled as the baby.

GOOD HOMES ARE ESSENTIAL

Planning

Before deciding to let your cat have kittens do try to be certain that you can find sufficient good homes for the new family, or if the kittens arrive unexpectedly, only keep as many as you are sure of being able to place. It is much kinder to ask your veterinary surgeon or local animal welfare clinic to destroy the unwanted kittens immediately after birth, rather than be left with the same sad problem when they are 7 to 8 weeks old.

Drowning kittens is not recommended as a means of disposal. It is neither quick nor humane even if they are only a few hours old. If you are quite unable to keep the litter it may be necessary to have them all put to sleep immediately after birth but there is no doubt that this causes the mother a great deal of distress and she may wander about for days looking for her lost family. There may also be some swelling or inflammation of the milk glands and if this is the case you should consult a veterinary surgeon. If just one kitten can be kept the mother cat will be

Spaying

content and it is best to arrange to have her neutered (or spayed, as it is called) as soon as the kitten is old enough to be left for a day (usually at about 4-5 weeks) to ensure that she does not become pregnant again.

15

SHOULD YOU LET YOUR CAT BREED?

There is no evidence at all to support the idea that it is better for a cat's health for her to have at least one litter of kittens. The neutered female is probably on average longer lived, requires less medical care and makes an ideal family pet.

THE BREEDING SEASON—OESTRUS OR CALLING

Female cats tend to come into season (or *calling* as it is known) from about 6 months old and they will, if allowed, become pregnant at this age, which is of course too young for their own welfare, since they are not fully grown and mature until 9 months-1 year.

Breeding times There are two main breeding periods:—The beginning of January—end of May and the beginning of July—end of August. Cats come into season less during the main winter months when the daylight hours are shorter but otherwise the times are rather variable and cannot be relied upon.

During the breeding period cats tend to come into season for 1-3 days at a time, at intervals of 14 days, but occasionally the season may last as long as 10 days. This makes it particularly difficult to ensure that if kittens are not wanted, the cat is kept in for the appropriate time.

BEHAVIOUR IN SEASON

Behaviour   Cats really do *call* when in oestrus. They develop a persistent and raucous voice, quite unlike their normal miaow and this is particularly noticeable in the Siamese. They become very restless and try to get out of the house at any opportunity and often at this time you will find that one or more unneutered tom cats have taken up residence in the garden. There is also a tendency for the females to roll about on their backs, giving the impression to inexperienced cat owners that they are in some acute pain.

PREVENTING SEASON

Family   The nuisance of the season problem can be reduced by means of an
planning   injection to prevent the season (see Chapter 3) but this is mainly of value to breeders who wish to postpone kittens until the cat is mature. For most households surgical sterilisation is the most satisfactory measure, at the present time.

Mating tends to be rather unintentional or unpremeditated in most cases for the family pet cat. If your cat gets out during the oestrus period she will almost certainly be mated and since ovulation appears to occur as a response to mating, the chances of conception are very high.

Under urban conditions where a female cat must be kept in because of traffic risk, it may be slightly more difficult if kittens are wanted. In this case it is probably best to consult the owner of a pedigree male cat who may be willing to arrange a mating (see Chapter 4, section on breeding and showing), or may know of someone who owns a crossbred unneutered male.

Usually if a cat has been mated, the symptoms of oestrus subside within 24 hours and do not recur, until about 5-6 weeks after the birth of its kittens. Cats are less likely to conceive while they are feeding their kittens but this is not by any means a reliable rule.

PREGNANCY

Gestation   Pregnancy usually lasts for 63-65 days, but of course except in the case of pedigree cats the exact date of mating is often uncertain (see table to calculate time).

RECOGNITION

3-5 weeks—your veterinary surgeon will be able to determine, as a rule, if your cat is in kitten by feeling the abdomen to detect the presence of the hard spherical foetuses (rather like marbles at this stage).

5-6 weeks—abdominal swelling may be noticed and there will be some enlargement of the milk glands.

8-9 weeks—the movements of the kittens may be noticed when the mother cat is relaxed.

However it often happens that all these signs are missed or mistaken for simple overweight and the first indication of pregnancy is the sound of kittens coming from the airing cupboard or some other unsuitable spot. This is even more surprising to owners who were certain that their cat was a tom.

A SUITABLE BED

Kittening   It is important to accustom your cat to sleeping in a special place that you have selected for the kittening at least one week before the kittens are due, or she may make her own plans to occupy the spare bed. If she is disturbed, or if for any reason she feels that the litter is in danger, a mother cat will sometimes transport her family for considerable distances, carrying each one in turn by the scruff of the neck.

A strong cardboard box is the best choice for a bed. Choose one which is large enough to accommodate the mother and her kittens comfortably and leave high sides, or a lid, to allow a sense of security and privacy. A step of several inches high should be left at the entrance side, to prevent adventurous tiny kittens wandering off into danger.

Keeping clean   Line the box with several layers of newspaper. Providing that the room itself is comfortably warm this will provide sufficient bedding during the birth and early days. Newspaper has the advantage that it can be removed in layers if necessary and burnt as it becomes soiled. It is less

PREGNANCY TABLE

Served January	Due to Kitten March	Served February	Due to Kitten April	Served March	Due to Kitten May	Served April	Due to Kitten June	Served May	Due to Kitten July	Served June	Due to Kitten August	Served July	Due to Kitten September	Served August	Due to Kitten October	Served September	Due to Kitten November	Served October	Due to Kitten December	Served November	Due to Kitten January	Served December	Due to Kitten February
1	5	1	5	1	3	1	3	1	3	1	3	1	2	1	3	1	3	1	3	1	3	1	2
2	6	2	6	2	4	2	4	2	4	2	4	2	3	2	4	2	4	2	4	2	4	2	3
3	7	3	7	3	5	3	5	3	5	3	5	3	4	3	5	3	5	3	5	3	5	3	4
4	8	4	8	4	6	4	6	4	6	4	6	4	5	4	6	4	6	4	6	4	6	4	5
5	9	5	9	5	7	5	7	5	7	5	7	5	6	5	7	5	7	5	7	5	7	5	6
6	10	6	10	6	8	6	8	6	8	6	8	6	7	6	8	6	8	6	8	6	8	6	7
7	11	7	11	7	9	7	9	7	9	7	9	7	8	7	9	7	9	7	9	7	9	7	8
8	12	8	12	8	10	8	10	8	10	8	10	8	9	8	10	8	10	8	10	8	10	8	9
9	13	9	13	9	11	9	11	9	11	9	11	9	10	9	11	9	11	9	11	9	11	9	10
10	14	10	14	10	12	10	12	10	12	10	12	10	11	10	12	10	12	10	12	10	12	10	11
11	15	11	15	11	13	11	13	11	13	11	13	11	12	11	13	11	13	11	13	11	13	11	12
12	16	12	16	12	14	12	14	12	14	12	14	12	13	12	14	12	14	12	14	12	14	12	13
13	17	13	17	13	15	13	15	13	15	13	15	13	14	13	15	13	15	13	15	13	15	13	14
14	18	14	18	14	16	14	16	14	16	14	16	14	15	14	16	14	16	14	16	14	16	14	15
15	19	15	19	15	17	15	17	15	17	15	17	15	16	15	17	15	17	15	17	15	17	15	16
16	20	16	20	16	18	16	18	16	18	16	18	16	17	16	18	16	18	16	18	16	18	16	17
17	21	17	21	17	19	17	19	17	19	17	19	17	18	17	19	17	19	17	19	17	19	17	18
18	22	18	22	18	20	18	20	18	20	18	20	18	19	18	20	18	20	18	20	18	20	18	19
19	23	19	23	19	21	19	21	19	21	19	21	19	20	19	21	19	21	19	21	19	21	19	20
20	24	20	24	20	22	20	22	20	22	20	22	20	21	20	22	20	22	20	22	20	22	20	21
21	25	21	25	21	23	21	23	21	23	21	23	21	22	21	23	21	23	21	23	21	23	21	22
22	26	22	26	22	24	22	24	22	24	22	24	22	23	22	24	22	24	22	24	22	24	22	23
23	27	23	27	23	25	23	25	23	25	23	25	23	24	23	25	23	25	23	25	23	25	23	24
24	28	24	28	24	26	24	26	24	26	24	26	24	25	24	26	24	26	24	26	24	26	24	25
25	29	25	29	25	27	25	27	25	27	25	27	25	26	25	27	25	27	25	27	25	27	25	26
26	30	26	30	26	28	26	28	26	28	26	28	26	27	26	28	26	28	26	28	26	28	26	27
27	31	27	May 1	27	29	27	29	27	29	27	29	27	28	27	29	27	29	27	29	27	29	27	28
28	Apr 1	28	2	28	30	28	30	28	30	28	30	28	29	28	30	28	30	28	30	28	30	28	Mar 1
29	2	29	3	29	31	29	Jly 1	29	31	29	31	29	30	29	31	29	Dec 1	29	31	29	31	29	2
30	3			30	Jne 1	30	2	30	Aug 1	30	Sep 1	30	Oct 1	30	Nov 1	30	2	30	Jan 1	30	Feb 1	30	3
31	4			31	2			31	2			31	2	31	2			31	2			31	4

dangerous than blankets, which may become wrapped around the young kittens causing suffocation.

Place the box in the quietest and most secluded area of the room. Mother cats much prefer to be left undisturbed in the early days to care for their family.

FEEDING DURING PREGNANCY

1. Up to 6 weeks

If your cat is receiving a sensible balanced diet it is not usually necessary to increase the volume of food during the first 5-6 weeks (see Chapter 4).

VITAMIN AND MINERAL SUPPLEMENTS

Correct diet

However it is important to ensure that the supply of essential vitamins and minerals is adequate to supply the needs of the developing kittens.

Vitamin A is important and can be supplied by adding raw liver to the diet twice or three times weekly. Sherley's Cod Liver Oil Capsules also provide a rich, natural source of Vitamin A.

Calcium

Calcium and phosphorus are needed for forming the bones of the developing embryos. They are present in milk or they may be supplied by feeding well-cooked fish and fish bone (although care must be taken to remove any large bones which have not softened. Cooking in a pressure cooker is best). Sherley's Calcium Tablets may also be given.

Sterilised bone flour can be added to the diet as a mineral supplement if deficiency of calcium and phosphorus is suspected. Your veterinary surgeon will advise on the appropriate amount to give, or may prescribe a compound vitamin and mineral tablet if this seems necessary. Sherley's Condition Tablets are a multi-vitamin and mineral supplement that can be used to provide a general addition to the diet.

2. From 6-9 weeks

At this stage the cat will probably develop a large appetite and the food can if required, be increased gradually to twice the normal quantity. It should preferably be divided into three or four meals to avoid abdominal discomfort.

EXERCISE

Tone

There is no need to place any special restrictions on the movements of the mother cat during pregnancy. In the earlier stages her usual activities will help to maintain muscle tone and in the later stages the weight of the kittens will probably slow her down quite sufficiently.

Care should be taken when picking her up to see that she is supported under the abdomen, to avoid any risk of twisting the uterus (or womb) in the later stages of pregnancy.

WORMING

Parasite
control

Under the influence of the hormones of pregnancy, round worms that have remained harmlessly encysted in the muscle become mature and may lead to a serious pre or post-natal infestation in the kittens, although the mother cat may have appeared to be quite free from worms. Treatment should be carried out in the last week of pregnancy, and at weekly intervals while feeding the kittens (see Chapter 5—Internal Parasites).

FLEAS

Young kittens are especially susceptible to fleas so giving the mother a dusting with an insecticidal powder in the last week of pregnancy is a wise precaution.

THE BIRTH

The process of birth is usually divided into 3 stages and as a rule mother cats will accomplish all these without any outside aid. However occasionally difficulties may arise, so it is as well just to peep into the box from time to time to be sure that all is proceeding according to plan (see later in chapter for possible complications).

First stage
of labour

When the birth is about to take place the cat will probably wander about and seem uneasy. She will often go in and out of the basket, sometimes *treading* the bedding, and making a loud purring sound. There may be a slight vaginal discharge and the body temperature at this time drops to below 100°F.

Second stage
of labour

There is definite straining and the cat may cry out, especially with a first litter. Usually after about 30 minutes the first kitten will appear at the vulva and will be expelled quite quickly. Sometimes the kitten will remain enveloped within the foetal membranes in a transparent sac, but as a rule the mother will break this at once and will start to lick and wash her kitten very vigorously to clean it and stimulate breathing. She will then bite through the umbilical cord and in a surprisingly short time the kitten will start to cry and then will make its way round to the milk glands, settling down contentedly to feed.

HEAD OR BREECH

Kittens may arrive normally by either the head, or breech (tail and hind feet) presentation. However in the case of a breech there is more risk of suffocation if the birth should be delayed.

Third stage
of labour

This is the expulsion of the afterbirth or placenta (the foetal membranes which connected the kitten to the blood supply of the mother by means of the umbilical cord). In most cases the kitten will be expelled still attached to the afterbirth and the mother will bite at the cord to sever it, then eat the membranes. This looks rather unpleasant but it is just how a cat would have behaved while living in the wild. It has been suggested that the afterbirth of the cat and the dog may contain hormones which are of value in the production of milk, or that they may have served as a source of protein in the first 48 hours after birth when the mother was reluctant to leave her young. However if too many are eaten they will probably cause vomiting and with a large litter it may be wise to remove any placentas that are seen and dispose of them.

Sometimes, since in the cat birth is a multiple process, stages 2 and 3 may tend to overlap, so that two or more kittens may be born, to be followed after an interval by the appropriate afterbirths. However if any afterbirths are retained they can cause infection and serious illness, so if you feel uncertain that this stage has been completed, or if your cat seems uneasy or unwell consult a veterinary surgeon.

Cutting the cord

It is rarely necessary to cut the cord since the mother does this job herself. However if after a period of about 10 minutes she has not done so and it becomes necessary, remember that hygiene is important. Scrub the hands with a disinfectant solution and apply a tight ligature (using boiled sewing thread) to the cord, several inches away from the kitten's abdomen. Using a pair of scissors sterilised by boiling, cut through the cord on the side away from the knot. The cord will shrivel and can be trimmed off later if necessary.

The number of kittens is as a rule from 3-7 (the average is 4).

The interval between the births varies from 10-60 minutes, though even longer delays may be quite normal if the cat is not straining hard or showing any signs of distress.

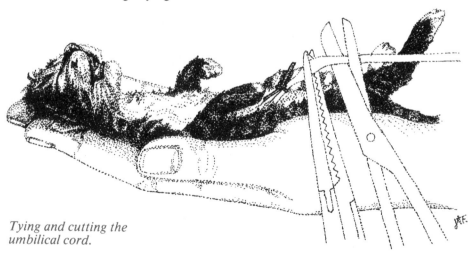

Tying and cutting the umbilical cord.

New-born kittens

Usually once the litter is complete, the mother cat will wash all her family and settle down to sleep. She will not as a rule take any food or drink during the birth but when it is over she will probably appreciate a drink of milk if it is offered to her in the bed. Some cats will refuse to leave their kittens at all during the first day, even for food. However, if possible they should be lifted out to relieve themselves, so that the bedding can be changed and the kittens checked for health.

PROBLEMS

When to call vet

Although kittening is usually easy and free from problems, troubles can occur and consulting a veterinary surgeon in good time may well save a life.

1. If your cat after straining for more than an hour has not managed to give birth, it is possible that there is a wrongly positioned kitten. This usually means that instead of lying in a stream-lined 'head first' or 'tail and hind feet first' position, the kitten is lying transversely across the neck of the uterus (or womb). This condition if not corrected, will be fatal, so get advice quickly.

Caesarean section

In cases where a cat is unable to produce her kitten because of wrong positioning, oversize, or other conditions, an operation (caesarean section) is usually required. If it is carried out in good time, before the mother has become exhausted the chances that she will recover and be able to rear her kittens are good.

The operation requires a general anaesthetic. The kittens are removed through a surgical wound in the middle of the abdomen, or on the flank, which is then closed with silk or nylon stitches (removed as a rule after 7 days). The veterinary surgeon may recommend sterilisation (neutering) at the same time, depending on the individual circumstances.

The cat will require warmth and careful nursing (see Chapter 6 for advice on care and feeding) but unless there are complications which endanger the life of the mother cat, she can as a rule be given her kittens immediately on recovery from the anaesthetic. They usually provide a considerable boost to her morale and will to live.

Large kittens

2. If an overlarge kitten has been partly expelled and then becomes wedged, it will usually be necessary to get veterinary assistance. However in an emergency the owner may be able to help, providing that the kitten is lying in a normal position. Check carefully that either the head and front legs are visible, or both hind feet and the tail. Grasp the kitten with a clean dry towel and as the cat strains, pull gently but firmly in a downward direction. If any doubt at all is felt about the position of the kitten, it should not be touched. A veterinary surgeon should be consulted as soon as possible.

Afterbirth

3. If you suspect that your cat has not expelled all the kittens or the afterbirths, or if she seems listless and unwilling to eat or care for the kittens, or if there is an excessive or unpleasant discharge from the vagina, or if she is running a temperature (see Chapter 8 for how to take a temperature), consult a veterinary surgeon at once. Antibiotic treatment may be needed to prevent the onset of a highly fatal septicaemia.

Mastitis

4. This may be indicated by hardness and swelling or discolouration of the milk glands. This will not only make the mother cat ill but will prevent her from feeding her kittens, so get advice quickly.

5. Prolapsed uterus—this is fortunately fairly uncommon. The mother

cat continues straining after the kittens are expelled and everts the uterus, which appears as a bloodstained spongey mass under the tail. This condition is extremely serious. Keep the patient in a clean warm spot (for instance on a clean cloth in a basket) and contact a veterinary surgeon as soon as possible.

REVIVING KITTENS

Sometimes after a delayed or difficult birth a kitten may appear to be dead but if a heart beat can be detected it is well worth attempting revival. Holding the kitten with the head slightly lower than the feet to allow any fluid to escape from the lungs, rub and massage the body with a warm dry towel. At intervals open the mouth (making sure that the tongue is depressed and not sticking to the roof of the mouth) and blow gently, to inflate the lungs and stimulate breathing. If any signs of life are seen, continue until the breathing becomes regular, then as soon as possible return the kitten to its mother.

ABNORMALITIES

Abnormal kittens

Before attempting to revive an apparently lifeless kitten, check that it is not suffering from any congenital abnormality. These may vary from kittens which are born with the muscular wall of the abdomen totally absent, to the less obvious but equally serious cleft palate which prevents the young animal from sucking and feeding. If kittens are born alive with any of these defects they should be taken to a veterinary surgeon as soon as possible to be humanely destroyed.

Remember of course that all kittens are born with their eyes closed and do not start to open them until they are about 12 days old.

THE NEW KITTENS

Sexing

Determining the sex of very young kittens is not easy but it may be of some consequence in deciding which kittens can be reared for potential homes. Your veterinary surgeon will certainly be able to help you if you have occasion to consult him, but otherwise you may be able to come to the right conclusion after reading the description in Chapter 3.

CARING FOR THE MOTHER CAT AND HER KITTENS

During the first 3-4 weeks of their lives the mother cat will care for her kittens completely. She will not only feed them but keep them scrupulously clean and by her constant licking ensure that bladder and bowels are functioning properly.

Feeding the mother

To supply the kittens' needs, without losing bodily condition, the food requirements of the mother cat are very high and she can be fed almost at will. At least three high protein meals (see Chapter 4 on Feeding) daily should be offered in addition to milk or Lactol. Fresh water should be available at all times as a high fluid intake is necessary to maintain the supply of milk for the family.

WEANING

To avoid excessive strain on the mother especially in the case of a large litter, it is advisable to start weaning the kittens from about 4 weeks old.

First foods

To tempt the kittens to try solid food, offer interesting flavours. Well stewed and shredded rabbit and chicken are usually popular, or shredded minced meat, boiled fish and well mashed canned meat or fish. Once the kittens have learned to lap, milk or Lactol should be offered three times daily.

Patience will be needed at first to persuade the kittens to feed. The food is best placed on a large flat plate. Try to ensure that each kitten gets a fair share and increase the amount gradually until by the age of 5 weeks you should be giving three to four meals daily (each kitten taking about 3oz daily of solid food in addition to milk). By 7-8 weeks old, the kittens should be independent of their mother and she will probably have started to get tired of her demanding family. It is best to provide an extra sleeping box on a higher level where she can retreat from time to time.

Season

Remember that at 5-6 weeks after the birth of the kittens the mother is likely to come into season, so she must be carefully watched if another litter of kittens is not to follow too soon.

CARING FOR ORPHAN KITTENS

To rear a large litter of orphan kittens is almost impossibly demanding for the average household. If the situation occurs every attempt should be made to find a foster mother. However in the case of just one or two kittens success is possible if the time can be sacrificed to give at least two weeks of constant care. The task can be a very rewarding one, since orphan kittens often grow up to be very strong healthy cats.

Warmth

Warmth is of the greatest importance—a room temperature of about 70°F is ideal. The box in which the kittens are kept should be placed close to a constant source of heat such as a radiator or boiler. A well wrapped hot water bottle should be placed in the box for the kittens to snuggle up to as a substitute mother.

The box should have high sides since tiny kittens are quite surprisingly active and adventurous. It should be lined with a thick layer of newspaper and on top of this a layer of blanket, or old quilt, for warmth.

Hygiene

To substitute for the constant licking action of the mother cat, the orphan kittens should be wiped all over after each meal with a warm damp flannel then thoroughly dried.

Health care

Constipation can usually be corrected by the addition of 2-3 drops of liquid paraffin to the milk mixture.

Diarrhoea is more serious and if the addition of a little powdered cornflour to the milk does not produce an improvement, a veterinary surgeon should be consulted, since dehydration (loss of body fluids) can very rapidly cause the death of young animals.

FEEDING

Lactol

Cow's milk alone is not sufficiently rich in protein, to act as substitute for the mother's milk. Sherley's Lactol is a complete milk food formulated to act as a replacement or supplement to the mother's milk.

Administration

Lactol can be given with either an eye dropper, or a Catac Foster Feeding Bottle but young kittens even though hungry are often reluctant to attempt to feed and endless patience will be needed. The Lactol mixture should be given at approx blood heat (101°F). Follow the mixing instructions on the Lactol tin.

Feed:— First 2 weeks every 2 hours.
Second 2 weeks every 4 hours.
Then every 6 hours.

How much?

Quantities will vary, but the kitten can be allowed as much as it is willing to take at each feed.

As a measure of progress, a healthy kitten should gain about 1/3 oz daily in weight and should double its birth weight in 8-9 days (kittens can be weighed weekly using kitchen scales).

Solid foods

Solid foods can be introduced from 3-4 weeks. Stewed meat or fish, finely shredded and mixed with gravy, and sieved meat or fish baby foods are ideal. The latter have the advantage that they can be given with a spoon as an introduction to new foods. Once the kitten has learned to lap, the task of feeding becomes much easier. Lactol can be continued in the diet and management can proceed as for the normal kitten.

The Catac Standard Foster Feeding Bottle produced by Cats Accessories Ltd., Newnham Street, Bedford.

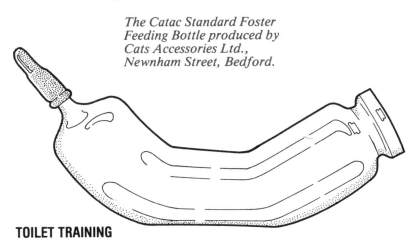

TOILET TRAINING

As soon as the kittens start to leave their mother they should be placed on the litter tray after every feed to start early house training. A clean kitten will be a particularly welcome arrival in its new home.

KITTEN HEALTH

Worming   Roundworms can constitute a danger to young kittens and even if the mother has been dosed, it is best to treat the kittens as well. Modern treatments are safe and palatable and do not require pre-fasting.

First dose   The first treatment can be given at from 4-5 weeks if worms are suspected and should be repeated at weekly intervals (see Chapter 5).

BEFORE YOUR KITTEN LEAVES HOME

Fleas, mites   Check for fleas and ear mites. Give your kitten a thorough overhaul for parasites before sending it to a new home (see Chapter 5 External Parasites).

VACCINATION AND NEUTERING

Stress to the new owners the importance of having kittens neutered and of vaccination against virus disease—see Chapter 3 (your veterinary surgeon may supply a leaflet on the subject), since the importance of preventative medicine does not always occur to the new cat owner.

It will also help if you give details of the type of food that you have used.

All these things will help to make your cat welcome in his new home and will ensure that he settles down happily with his new owners.

CARING FOR YOUR NEW KITTEN

CHOOSING A KITTEN

It is probably true to say that, while acquiring a puppy is usually a deliberate choice, choosing (or being chosen by) a cat is often accidental. Sometimes a homeless kitten arrives in the garden, or a neighbour is anxious to find homes for an unplanned litter, or one hears that a kitten will be put to sleep unless a home is found at once. Almost without premeditation one becomes a cat owner. However it is important to check first that the whole family agree to the new arrival. It is not fair through an impulse of generosity to bring a kitten into a house where it is not really welcome. To provide a home is not enough. Quite a lot of love and care will be needed as well.

THE RIGHT AGE

8 weeks
best

Ideally kittens should be 8 weeks old before they are sent to a new home, or if younger, they should be completely weaned and used to sleeping away from the mother cat. A kitten of 4-5 weeks old, which has not learned to lap or to take sufficient solid food on its own to maintain life, has a very poor chance of survival in the outside world. However the arrival of a kitten is not always premeditated or arranged. If your new pet looks much younger and smaller than you had expected it will need special care in the first few days if it is to develop into a healthy young cat.

WHERE TO GET YOUR KITTEN

A home
you know

The healthiest kittens are as a rule those that come from good private homes. They have had the advantage of proper feeding during their first weeks of life and a relatively low risk of contact with outside infections. Even more important, a kitten from a kind and loving home which is used to being handled by people is more likely to have an even temperament and be free from excessive nervousness. It should be easier to feed (especially if you check with the owner as to previous types and times of feeding). It may even be house-trained, at least to some extent.

If you do not know of any kittens in your immediate circle, try asking at your local corner shop, where this kind of information is often to be found. Alternatively look in your local, or evening paper. Kittens are often advertised as *free to good homes.*

Cats' Homes
It is certainly an act of kindness to give a home to a kitten from a Cats' Home but it is not always a venture with a happy ending. Young kittens which have been handed into a shelter at 5-6 weeks old have very little resistance and in this situation there is every chance that they will come in contact with infection (most commonly the 'flu or enteritis viruses). A kitten which appears quite healthy to you, or to the home official who hands it out, may well be in the incubating stages of disease. The recovery rate for very young kittens is not good. For your new pet to die within a week or two can be a most upsetting experience for children in the family—and for adults too.

Pet shops
Likewise, care is also needed when buying a kitten from a pet shop. Make sure that the shop has a good source of kittens and a high standard of hygiene. The kitten you choose should be lively and healthy.

PEDIGREE CATS

Breeders
When buying a pedigree cat the same rules apply. A long pedigree and a high price are no guarantee of health, so wherever possible collect your kitten directly from the breeder and find out as much as possible about its background. A reliable breeder will as a rule agree to let your own veterinary surgeon examine the kitten for health before you complete the purchase. It is in the best interests of breeders' reputations to sell only sound kittens and they are usually glad to know that the animals which they have reared are going to caring homes.

BUYER BEWARE

Never on any account buy a kitten unseen from an advertisement. A young animal which is sent by train may easily suffer as a result of unexpected and even unavoidable delays. Even if it is sold under a *money back if not satisfactory* arrangement, you may be involved in considerable trouble or even heartbreak if your new pet does not match up to the advertisement.

Choosing
your cat
There is, nowadays, a great number of different pedigree cats to choose from (see Chapter 1), although Siamese in their various varieties are probably top favourites. These cats have been carefully selected and bred and their price will vary with their rarity and their show potential. For the cat lover, breeding and showing can provide an interesting hobby. The best way to learn about cats and to choose your favourite kind is to visit your local cat show (see Chapter 4). However, unless you really have a lot of time to spare avoid the long-haired Persian varieties.

The enchantingly pretty fluffy kittens which are so often i͟
advertisements, are only kept this way by constant care and a n͟
and tangled Persian soon becomes a misery to itself.

PEDIGREE CROSS KITTENS

Half-bred

Half-bred pedigree kittens (usually the result of the accidental mating of a Siamese, or other type of pedigree cat) are sometimes offered for sale or free to good homes. While they do not as a rule follow the colour of the pedigree they do have many of the breed characteristics, and make very attractive pets.

CROSS-BREDS

While the various pedigree cats are very attractive, they have no monopoly of charm and intelligence. Whether your cross-bred cat is handsome, pretty or just unusual, it is fairly certain that you will think that it is the best in the world.

MALE OR FEMALE

The sex of the new kitten is not as a rule of great consequence if it is to be a family pet, since most thoughtful owners will probably decide on neutering in either case (see section on neutering later in this chapter). The temperaments and characters of the neutered male and female are very similar. The female may, marginally, be sweeter and more affectionate and the male may, just marginally, be more independent but these are only generalisations and many owners would probably disagree.

Male or female

It is not easy for the average person to distinguish the sex of a very young kitten, in fact many kittens are booked in for neutering under the wrong sex, to the great surprise of the owner who was quite certain that their *female* was a *tom*, or vice versa.

SEX LINKED COLOURS

Colours

In some cases the sex of the cat can be surmised from its colour. True tortoiseshells are always female (but doubt sometimes arises as to identification of this colour—a particular mixture of reddish brown and black hairs).

Ginger cats are often (but not always) males. Contrary to popular opinion, ginger females are not sterile and can breed successfully.

White cats

However it is true that in some cases an all white colour in cats is linked with deafness. This can be a great disadvantage since a deaf cat is exposed to dangers—both from traffic and animal enemies.

IDENTIFICATION

To attempt to identify the sex of your new kitten, first stand *it* on a table, in a good light and lift up the tail.

29

the male the uro-genital opening is a small circular dot below and
ghtly separated from the anus, rather like a colon (:). It may also be
ossible to see the slight swelling of the testicles, just below the lower
pening.

*Sexing kittens: the female
is on the left and the male
on the right.*

In the female the opening (vulva) is in the same situation, below but
closer to the anus and is rather more elongated vertically, like an inverted
exclamation mark (see diagram). When looking at a male and female
kitten together the differences are fairly obvious but considering one on
its own can be puzzling, especially when they are very young.

WHETHER PEDIGREE OR CROSS-BRED—A HEALTHY KITTEN IS THE IMPORTANT CHOICE

A litter of young kittens is a very attractive sight and to most prospective cat owners the temptation is strong to choose the one which
looks the prettiest and take it home at once. However a little time spent
on checking over the proposed new addition to the family may save some
trouble and worry in the weeks to come.

GENERAL APPEARANCE

Bright and active

A healthy kitten should be bright, active and interested in the world around it. One that is very shy, or inclined to back into a corner and spit at strangers may have a difficult temperament and grow up to be a problem cat.

Plumpness is a healthy sign but an over-distended stomach in proportion to the body may indicate poor feeding, or the presence of roundworms (see Chapter 5).

Coat

The coat should be shiny, clean and free from parasites, although even in the best of homes the occasional flea may be found. However this is not a serious problem and it is a good precaution to give any new kitten a dusting with a suitable insecticidal powder on arrival in the new home (see Chapter 5—External Parasites).

Ears

The ears should be examined for the hard crusty deposits in the ear canal, which indicate the presence of ear mites (see Chapter 5—External Parasites). This condition can certainly be cured by the application of suitable drops such as Sherley's Canker Lotion Capsules, but a severe infestation can make a young kitten quite ill and it is probably best to ask the owner to carry out treatment before taking the kitten home.

The healthy kitten has clear bright eyes and an only slightly moist and pinkish nose.

Eyes and nose

Beware of the so called *cold*. Cats do not get the trivial common cold as humans do and any sneezing, or discharge from the eyes or nose must be taken as a danger signal. It may be a symptom of the onset of cat 'flu (see Chapter 7), a virus disease which can be very serious and fatal, or it may indicate that the kitten has chronic catarrh, a condition which, while it rarely kills, can be a recurring nuisance throughout life. In some areas, especially on farms, this condition may be found in nearly all the cats, which have continuously runny eyes and noses, together with sneezing and catarrhal symptoms. They are often permanently stunted as a result.

Having said all this, it is a fact that many cats arrive unexpectedly in the home, sometimes in poor condition as a result of straying and exposure. Check through all the previous points and also consider whether there is any sign of diarrhoea, or if the kitten seems unable to take food. Young animals have very little resistance to infection and if they are unable to feed, quickly become dehydrated and weak. In these circumstances it is important to take the kitten to your own veterinary surgeon or to an animal welfare clinic as soon as possible for examination and treatment.

BRINGING HOME THE NEW KITTEN

Cat box

When collecting your new kitten remember that he, or she may well be frightened by the first contact with the noisy outside world (and nervous kittens are inclined to bolt), so it is important to take a strong carrying box of some kind. If you have a proper cat box this is of course ideal.

If you decide to buy one, it will certainly be of use in the future if your cat has to travel, or even for necessary visits to the vet (see Chapter 4—Caring for the Adult Cat, for more information on this subject). If you do not want to go to this expense you will probably find that your local Animal Welfare Society (RSPCA or PDSA) sells strong cardboard cat carriers quite cheaply. These are very suitable for transporting kittens, though they may not be adequate for a boisterous adult cat.

As an emergency cat box, two strong cardboard boxes can be used (after making ventilation holes), the larger fitting completely over the smaller to form a lid and being tied around with string (see diagram). This may seem an unnecessary amount of caution but nothing could be sadder than to lose a young kitten in a strange area through lack of taking care.

Finally, a warm blanket in the box will be comforting, especially if the weather is cold.

An emergency cat box
made by fitting a large over
a smaller box.

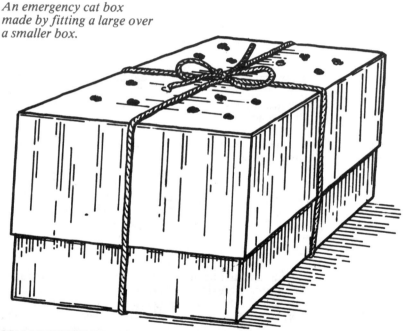

COLLAR AND NAME TAG

It is a good idea to buy a proper cat collar (with an elasticated safety section to avoid the risk of strangulation if he should become entangled in a tree) as soon as you get your new kitten and to have a disc made with your name, address and telephone number. It is only too easy for young animals to stray and your chances of recovering your new pet will be much greater if he can be easily identified.

Many Siamese cats learn to walk on collar and lead like dogs. This idea could quite usefully be applied to other breeds, giving a little more mobility and safety to strange situations such as when travelling.

THE NEW HOME

Taking care

Cats are inquisitive animals and your new kitten will certainly want to get out of the basket and make a thorough inspection of his new surroundings, so make certain that all doors and windows are shut. Also, if there is an open fire or fire grate, make certain that there is a guard in place because timid kittens have been known to bolt up chimneys. It is really best to confine the newcomer at first to one room as far as possible, until he has become accustomed to the place. He will probably not be house-trained and this will minimise the risk of accidents occurring on carpets. It is also for his own safety, since tiny kittens can so easily be stepped on and injured when they are encountered unexpectedly.

FREEDOM OR SAFETY—WHEN TO LET YOUR NEW KITTEN OUT

This is always a very difficult decision to take and depends upon the individual circumstances. At least one week should be allowed for the kitten to adapt to his surroundings and for the sights, sounds and smells which make up the new home to become imprinted on his mind. If you have a well enclosed garden you may then decide to let him out for a stroll and an investigation, but only under supervision.

TRAFFIC DANGERS

Traffic

If you live near a busy road you may have to decide to keep your cat in altogether.

Unfortunately there is no way of preventing a cat from straying into danger. If you allow your cat to go out alone in an area where there is heavy traffic, you must face the fact that he will probably one day be injured or killed.

GOING OUT AT NIGHT

Cats in the wild were probably, at least partly nocturnal animals and on summer nights they love to stay out chasing moths and other big game. However the danger from traffic at night is even greater than by day, since cats are often injured after being dazzled by car headlights and there is always the thought that a pet may be lying hurt for some hours before he is found. Under today's conditions it is probably kinder and wiser to keep cats in unless you live in a very rural area.

Partial freedom

As a compromise it is worth considering constructing a wire netting enclosure in the garden for your kitten. If it is furnished with an old tree branch as a seat and a place to scratch the claws, it will provide a little fresh air and exercise together with peace of mind for the owner. The cat run need not be large but it should be strongly made. Choose an area which has some shade as well as sunshine and provide a box or shelter to give protection from rain if your cat is to be left for some hours at a time.

BUTTERING THE PAWS

There was an old superstition that buttering the paws prevented a new kitten from straying away. There is certainly no basis in fact for this at all but perhaps people thought that a cat that was cleaning butter off his feet would be too busy to stray.

MEETING THE CHILDREN

Introductions   Children usually love kittens and kittens thoroughly enjoy being played with and encouraged to chase a piece of paper or string but it is important to teach the children that pets are not just toys but must be allowed plenty of time to sleep and rest when the games are over. Allowing an older child to be responsible for the cat's feeding and grooming will do much to encourage a love and a sense of responsibility for pets.

MEETING OTHER FAMILY PETS

Introducing your new kitten to cats or dogs who are already established in the household may present problems. Prepare to face a certain amount of illwill and try to minimise jealousy by not making too much fuss over the newcomer. With cats, after a day or two of spitting and growling at the new member of the family, things usually settle down and after the initial strangeness has warn off they quite obviously enjoy the company of one of their own kind and get much more fun out of life. Having said this however there are occasionally cases where cats prove to be completely incompatible and the only kind solution is to try to find another home for the newcomer.

Meeting dogs   In the case of a dog which is not accustomed to cats it is obviously necessary to take more care. Many dogs have a strong hunting instinct, regarding any small animal that runs away as a legitimate quarry. A young kitten might easily be injured or even killed in the first few moments. Even if they appear to have accepted each other, it is not wise to leave a dog alone with a young kitten for any time or to feed the two together. However, once friendship becomes established, cats and dogs usually get on very well together, often sharing the same basket and washing each other, although the dog may still feel justified in chasing other people's cats. Indeed it is true to say that in most homes in the end it is the cat who seems to rule the roost.

HIS OWN CORNER AND HIS OWN BED

Warmth is of the greatest importance in the care of young animals and in winter it is best to keep your kitten in a constant, even, warm temperature away from draughts (ideally in the kitchen). If the bed or box is placed against a radiator, stove, or other source of heat the newcomer will as a rule adopt it as his own and settle down very comfortably to sleep.

Bed or box?   A bed of his own gives a great sense of security to a kitten in a strange new home.

A cardboard box with one side cut down to provide a step, and the other sides left high to keep out draughts is very suitable, or you can place the box on its side to provide a completely roofed house. These have the great advantage of being inexpensive, and easy to replace. However if you or your cat would like something a little more elaborate, there are many different types of bed to be found nowadays at pet stores, from the traditional basketwork, to the modern polystyrene shape with a plastic cover (these latter have the advantage of being easily sponged clean) but as a general rule a cat will feel safer and more content in a bed with high sides.

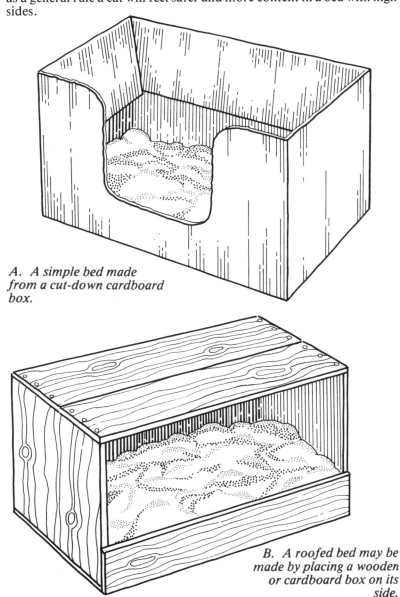

A. A simple bed made from a cut-down cardboard box.

B. A roofed bed may be made by placing a wooden or cardboard box on its side.

BLANKETS AND BEDDING

Cats love comfort and they will appreciate a pillow or a blanket in their bed, often quite visibly expressing their pleasure at new soft bedding by treading, or kneading the ground and purring loudly. However it is best to use either a polystyrene foam square, covered by a blanket, or a plastic cushion, since flock or feather pillows may harbour fleas. The bed covers should be washed regularly, or alternatively you can use pieces of old quilted dressing gowns, or other remnants which can be discarded and burnt.

FEEDING KITTENS

Proper diet

The kitten has a very high dietary requirement compared to the adult cat. Because it is growing fast it needs food not only to supply body heat and energy but also to form tissues and bones. In fact a kitten of 7 weeks old may well eat the equivalent of 20% of its own body weight in food each day.

Meat

Cats are naturally total carnivores (meat eaters) and have a very high requirement of protein and fat in the diet. In the wild state this would be totally supplied by the consumption of birds, mice, rabbits and other small mammals which form their prey. It is also worth noting that in the wild, cats probably took very little water as such (they were originally desert dwellers) since fresh animal carcasses contain approximately 90% of fluid and this supplied sufficient for their needs. Carbohydrate is not a normal constituent of the diet of the cat, since they use protein to supply energy but it can be used as a food supplement to supply bulk if given in conjunction with a high protein food.

VITAMINS AND MINERALS

Balanced diet

Cats have a rather higher requirement of Vitamins, A, D, and B12 than other animals, and calcium is especially required by the growing kitten and the pregnant cat. However all these elements will be found in adequate amounts in a normal balanced diet and harm can be caused by over-administration of vitamins. If you suspect that your kitten may be suffering from a deficiency condition it is safest to consult a veterinary surgeon or animal welfare clinic rather than attempt to remedy the situation yourself before diagnosis.

WHEN TO FEED

At first, *little and often* is the best rule.

A General Guide

Age	Total daily amount of a high protein food (canned or fresh)		Number of meals
7-12 weeks	3-5 oz	divided into	4
3 months-6 months	5-7 oz	divided into	3
6 months-1 year	7-7½ oz	divided into	2

Lactol or milk may be given in addition to stated amounts.

Feeding guide The table given above is intended only as a general guide and the amounts of food mentioned are average figures. Individual animals may vary considerably in their food requirements, not only according to their age, health and the conditions of their life but also according to their metabolic rate (that is the rate at which each animal converts food into heat and energy). If you feel unhappy about your kitten's growth or progress always consult your own veterinary surgeon or visit your nearest animal welfare clinic for advice.

FOOD TO USE

FRESH FOODS

Protein and fat are supplied by all fresh meats and offals. Lungs (lights) can be used occasionally but they have a poor food content and while they are obviously palatable and very popular with cats, they are not really suitable for growing kittens: also buy fish (tinned and fresh), rabbit, chicken, chicken giblets, etc.

Cheese is a good source of protein and is well accepted by many cats.

Milk (as fresh milk or Lactol) is a good source of protein and also of calcium and Vitamin D. However milk soon deteriorates if it is left in the dish, so if your kitten does not finish the drink, take it up and throw it away.

Allergy
Very occasionally cats show an allergic reaction to cow's milk, resulting in diarrhoea or skin irritation. If you suspect this consult a veterinary surgeon.

PREPARED MANUFACTURED FOODS

Nowadays the majority of cats are fed on convenience manufactured foods (This subject is covered more fully in Chapter 4—Caring for the Adult Cat). Dried foods, although they are designed as a total food are probably better used only as a dietary supplement for the young cat because of the difficulties which can arise as a result of their very low fluid intake. However, the canned and semi-moist foods prepared by the leading manufacturers are very carefully formulated to provide a balanced food, with the appropriate vitamins and minerals. If given in accordance with the instructions, they should provide a suitable diet for a normal kitten. They are as a rule very palatable and have the great advantage of being readily available and easy to prepare.

Tinned, dry, or semi-moist

If wished, fresh, or raw foods can be used to supplement a diet of prepared foods but there is no evidence to show that this is necessary.

Water
Although the water consumption of some cats is very low, water should be available at all times and it is especially important in hot weather, or if a dry, or semi-moist food is being used.

Bones
Young kittens thoroughly enjoy having a bone to chew and a large beef bone will keep them occupied and amused for hours. Avoid all small bones as these may cause choking.

FEEDING THE NEW ARRIVAL

When your new kitten arrives he may feel strange and uncertain in his new surroundings or he may be unused to the type of food which you are offering. The best policy is to offer not more than a teaspoonful of some very palatable food on a saucer (well-cooked and boned rabbit, cooked giblets, or white fish are all highly acceptable as a rule) and to wait until this has been finished before offering more. It is better that the kitten should be slightly under, rather than over-fed, until it has adjusted to the new routine.

For the very young kitten, sieved baby foods (meat or fish) can be used and can be given with a spoon if necessary.

The right amount

Once a satisfactory feeding routine has been established, make it a rule to put down the amount of food that you expect to be eaten at each feeding time and if it is not all cleared up, promptly remove it until the next meal is due. If your kitten seems perfectly fit and playful and yet food is being left at each meal, you are probably over-estimating his, or her requirements and you should reduce the amount of each meal accordingly.

Healthy cats do not simply become bored with a food that they have previously enjoyed unless they are being overfed, so avoid falling into the trap of searching for new foods to tempt the jaded appetite of a cat who has already eaten quite enough. And finally, don't leave a plate of biscuits down to be nibbled at will throughout the day. This is an ideal way to spoil the appetite for cats—or humans.

FEEDING DISHES

In the interest of hygiene your kitten should have his own feeding dishes which are kept separate. Old saucers will certainly serve the purpose but the plastic dishes sold at pet stores (in a non-tip over design) are inexpensive and since they are unbreakable, last for years.

WARNING

Dehydration

Young kittens which arrive at their new home in the early stages of gastro-enteritis infection may refuse to eat any food and if not given prompt veterinary treatment will probably quickly become dehydrated and weak. They may die. If you suspect that this may be the case with your new kitten, consult a veterinary surgeon as soon as possible. In the meantime keep the patient very warm and try to give a few drops of milk, Lactol, or meat broth every hour with a dropper (see Chapter 6 on Treatment and First Aid).

TRAINING

Cats are not as a rule as easily trained as dogs. They have a greater sense of independence and are less concerned with pleasing their owners. Sometimes a battle of wills may be needed before a satisfactory code of behaviour is established. Remember that your cat will be a much more enjoyable member of the family if he has learned some basic good manners. However since cats do not bark at night or bite the neighbours, or chew up shoes, they do start with some built-in advantages.

TOILET TRAINING

This is the first and most important lesson if your cat is to have the freedom of the house.

Taught by mother

Cats are naturally very clean animals and some kittens (especially those that have remained with the mother cat to the age of 8 weeks or more) may have already acquired some idea of house-training before they reach their new home. If your kitten is among this number you are very lucky.

However in the case of kittens which have been living wild, or have had several unsatisfactory homes the situation is very different and unfortunately bad habits, once learned, can be hard to lose.

Patience is essential

Patience is the most important factor in training or in re-training a cat. They are timid animals and if you become angry and shout, or hit your cat for soiling the floors you may simply create a neurotic pet who will never fully recover its confidence in the world.

TRAY OR GARDEN

In almost all cases it is necessary to train a cat at first to use a litter tray, even if you hope later to let it use the garden. If you are a keen gardener yourself (or even more important, if your neighbours are) it may be worthwhile continuing to empty a tray once or twice daily, rather than have the nuisance and the problem that results from having a cat dig up gardens. In any case, in bad weather or through the night a tray will be necessary for the first few weeks and it can be a great help when moving house, or putting a cat into kennels if he is still accustomed to using a tray.

There are two very important rules to observe in training a cat to be house clean:

Two rules

1. See that he is confined to one room only until the idea of using the litter tray is thoroughly imprinted on his mind.

Young animals have only very limited control over bladder and bowels and if a kitten is allowed the freedom of the house, or is shut in a room with carpets for some hours accidents can be expected; and once carpets have become soiled with urine, cats, like puppies, have a tendency to assume that this is an appropriate place and return to it. If the kitten is kept in one room with an impervious floor which can be properly washed and disinfected the nuisance will be kept to a minimum.

2. Provide a suitable litter tray. See that it remains always in the same place (preferably a quiet corner of the kitchen) and see that the litter is changed as often as necessary. Cats are very fastidious animals and are

reluctant to use a soiled tray. Once clean habits are established it may be possible to remove the tray from the kitchen to a garage or basement if preferred but beware of upsetting your cat's routine too soon.

Litter trays A metal or plastic (and therefore waterproof) tray is ideal—an old baking tin with a depth of about 2″ can be used, or an old enamel or fibreglass tray. If none of these is available in the home a proper litter tray can be bought at most pet stores. This should be lined with a strong layer of newspaper and then given a good scattering of earth, ashes, sand or preferably one of the prepared cat litter products which contain a deodorising agent and are much less unpleasant in a kitchen. Some cats are inclined to scratch rather vigorously in their litter, scattering it on the floor, so it may be a good idea to place the tray in a large flat cardboard box lid to reduce the mess. The tray should be washed with a disinfectant solution each week.

Put the kitten on to the tray after every meal, whenever it wakes up, or at any other time when you think it may be necessary. Sherley's Swiftie trainer sprinkled in the tray often helps to start the right habit.

If the kitten makes a mess elsewhere in the room, take it to the spot and reprimand it in a very cross tone of voice, but without shouting. It is not necessary to smack a cat (your meaning will be quite clear) but you can if you like tap sharply on your hand, or against the furniture with a rolled newspaper. Cats very much dislike the sound and soon learn to associate it with a rebuke.

Garden Having once trained your cat to use a tray it can sometimes be difficult to retrain it to use the garden, especially in cold weather. However in most cases with the return of summer, when the cat can spend long hours in the garden the problem usually resolves of its own accord, although it may sometimes help if the litter tray is placed outside the back door for a while.

TRAINING YOUR KITTEN TO COME WHEN CALLED

This is an important lesson but it is not by any means as easy as when training a puppy. The psychology of the cat is very different; he does not respond automatically to the sound of the owner's voice but quite sensibly makes a reasoned judgement as to whether it is in his own interest to come at that time.

Rewards However, much can be done to induce a reflex tendency to come when called by the use of rewards. Find something that your cat really enjoys, perhaps a meaty biscuit, or a tiny piece of cheese and he will soon come to associate the particular tone of your voice when you call with the treat to come (and it is of course important always to give the treat if the system is to work). This habit when once established can save a great deal of annoyance on those occasions when it is essential to get your cat in a hurry. However be warned, it will not work well with the overfed cat, or the one which is allowed to pick at food all day.

Do train your cat not to sit on furniture. It can be done if you start out with determination and check him every time he tries to get on a chair.

He has his own comfortable bed, so there is no need to feel sorry for him and it is not pleasant to find that clothes are covered with cat hair.

If your will power is not quite up to this at least make sure that your cat sleeps in just one chair in the house.

Claws

The bad habit which causes the most annoyance to owners is scratching or clawing at furniture, carpets and even sometimes wallpaper. Siamese are probably the worst culprits (and they have very strong nails) and with an adult cat the habit may well prove incurable. It is particularly difficult because to the cat his behaviour is a perfectly normal method of sharpening the claws and he probably finds it odd that his owner objects so much. Boredom is probably the main cause of this type of destructiveness. A cat which has a garden to wander in and trees to climb usually learns to sharpen his claws in the outside world but this of course is of little comfort to the flat dweller with a well loved but destructive pet.

Scratching post

With a young kitten every possible effort must be made to let him know that this behaviour is unacceptable. Check him at once if he is caught in the act (using the rolled paper method again to make a loud noise—this is even a case when a quick tap with the paper might be justified since the lesson really must be learned). See that the nails are not allowed to grow too long. Cut just the tips yourself with nail clippers, or if you feel uncertain of how to do this, visit your veterinary surgeon or animal welfare clinic and ask to be shown (see also Nails in Chapter 4—Adult Cat). Provide a scratching post. Either use a fallen tree bough which you may perhaps keep in the garage or the kitchen, or buy a prepared scratching post from a pet shop. These are impregnated with a substance which is attractive to cats and are sometimes more successful for this reason but you can construct one yourself with wood and a thick strip of carpet.

As far as possible see that your cat is not left alone in rooms where there is furniture to damage. Unfortunately it can sometimes prove impossible to keep a really destructive cat.

CLAW REMOVAL

Painless

As a last resort for cats which are incurably destructive, it is worth considering having the claws surgically removed. Many owners feel reluctant to take this step, but the operation is quite painless (it is carried out under general anaesthesia) and in the USA where it is widely practised it is noticed that the cats do not seem to suffer any untoward consequences and do not even lose their ability to climb trees. However it does have the disadvantage of leaving a cat with reduced defences against other felines or dogs.

GROOMING

As soon as you bring home your new fluffy kitten you should also buy a brush and comb and establish a regular grooming routine, once weekly for short-haired varieties and daily for Persian and other long hairs (see also Chapter 4—Caring for the Adult Cat). A strong nylon hairbrush and a fine comb (either steel or plastic) are essential tools. Spread a thick layer of newspaper on a table in a good light, and apart from combing out tangles, check the following:—

1. Check the eyes and nose for any discharge. Staining around the eyes is sometimes a problem with white cats. Consult your veterinary surgeon if there is any redness, soreness or excessive watering. Stains can be removed with Sherley's Tear Stain Remover.
2. Check the ears for the presence of dark wax which may denote the presence of ear mites (see Chapter 5) or any discharge.
3. Check the coat for fleas, lice or ticks (see Chapter 5).
4. Check the nails; if too long the ends may be just *tipped* with nail cutters.

Grooming should not be an ordeal which your cat dreads provided you approach it sensibly. Spend a little time combing the ticklish areas under the chin and behind the ears (which they usually enjoy) as well as carrying out the more serious work.

MEDICAL CARE

Worms

Young kittens generally have roundworms and less frequently, tapeworms. See Chapter 5 for details of recognition and treatment and other parasites including fleas, lice, ear mites etc.

TEETHING—See Chapter 7

VACCINATION

Feline enteritis

1. Enteritis vaccination has been carried out for a number of years and appears to provide an effective level of immunity against virus gastroenteritis, a very serious and often fatal disease characterised by high temperature, vomiting and diarrhoea (see Chapter 7). It is a condition which is encountered most in boarding kennels, or breeding catteries and for this reason some proprietors of catteries insist on a certificate of vaccination before admitting cats for boarding.

Vaccination is by injection and is usually carried out from 9 weeks old. Booster injections are necessary. It is not as a rule carried out at welfare clinics (because of the cost) so consult a private veterinary surgeon.

Influenza

2. Vaccination against cat influenza has been introduced fairly recently, and appears to be giving very good results. The method is by injection or by droplet inhalation. Since this serious, and often fatal, disease occurs most often in catteries and kennels, vaccination is strongly advised for anyone who may have to board their pet during holidays. Remember to consult your veterinary surgeon in good time to obtain maximum protection.

NEUTERING—PREVENTING THE CAT POPULATION EXPLOSION

Many new cat owners may feel reluctant to consider having their kitten neutered but there really are very sound reasons in favour, both for the male and the female.

THE FEMALE CAT

The female cat will, if allowed, have several litters each year, often becoming pregnant again before she has finished feeding the last litter. One cat may in her own life time be responsible for hundreds of offspring. Apart from the fact that this overproduction exhausts the mother cat and shortens her life, there simply are not sufficient kind and caring homes to take in all these newcomers. No cat lover would want to bring kittens into the world to end as hungry and unwanted strays.

OESTRUS OR SEASON

Calling

The female kitten comes into season (or *calling* as it is known, because she really does develop a very loud and persistent miaow, quite different from the usual sound) at 6 months or soon after. If allowed out she will almost certainly become pregnant. Keeping a cat in at this time is far from easy, since she of course is determined to get out and may become very irritable and even bad tempered. Worse still you will usually find that several of the local tom cats have arrived on the door step, or even in the house, if they have the opportunity.

THE OPERATION

Neutering or spaying involves a surgical operation, under general anaesthetic, to remove both the uterus and the ovaries and prevent the cat from coming into season or becoming pregnant again.

Age

It is usually carried out from 12 weeks onwards. Opinions vary slightly as to the best time, so consult your own veterinary surgeon. If you have decided not to breed, before 6 months is safest to avoid the risk of pregnancy. However if you decide you would like to rear one litter the operation can be carried out later and as a rule it causes the cat remarkably little distress or disturbance.

In most instances you will be asked to bring your kitten to the veterinary surgeon first thing in the morning, after having starved her for at least 12 hours (this is to avoid the risk of vomiting under an anaesthetic) and may be able to collect her the same evening or on the following day. Your own veterinary surgeon will give you more precise instructions if you ask but as a rule, with a little extra care and attention for the first day or two, your kitten will soon be her playful self again.

Owners are sometimes distressed when a cat returns looking dazed, or behaving in an uncoordinated way but this is of course perfectly normal after a general anaesthetic. It is best to keep the patient in a confined space (ideally in a cat basket) and in a warm atmosphere for the first few hours.

Feeding

Do not be in too much hurry to offer food. Many cats arrive home feeling fit and hungry and demand their meal, but it is usually best to offer either warm milk, or an absolute minimum of food. Over-eating may lead to vomiting and that is both painful and dangerous after an abdominal operation.

In most cases the female cat will have one or more stitches, either on the flank, or under the abdomen, which the veterinary surgeon will remove after 7 days. Cats are much less inclined than dogs to remove their own stitches but they should if possible be prevented from biting or pulling at them. It may in some cases be necessary to construct a cotton jacket to cover the stitches since it is not easy to keep an abdominal bandage on a cat.

CHEMOTHERAPEUTIC METHODS

Oestrus and pregnancy can be prevented or postponed by means of a chemical given by injection or tablet. This is helpful for an owner who thinks that they might like to have a litter at some more convenient time, or who is very reluctant to face the thought of an operation. However the treatment must be repeated at intervals of 6 months or 1 year throughout life and for the average owner it is not as satisfactory or as free from complications as the surgical method.

THE MALE CAT

Male cats are neutered partly for their own welfare and partly to make them more suitable as household pets.

Mature male cats tend to wander away in search of females, sometimes becoming lost and ending up as strays and frequently being injured or killed on roads. They have a strong instinct to fight other males in their territory and as a consequence suffer severe wounds and abscesses, often looking battered and battle scarred before they are more than two years old.

There is also the disadvantage from the owner's point of view, that the urine of the unneutered male develops a characteristically strong, unpleasant and persistent odour. In the breeding season even house-trained males are liable to urinate or *spray* in their own homes.

Neutering is a simple operation in the male. It is carried out under general anaesthetic and is usually free from side effects.

The operation is usually carried out at from 3-8 months although adult males may also be neutered. At the younger age the operation is scarcely noticed but some opinions favour waiting until the cat is more mature. While the operation is not generally an abdominal one, the cat may feel a little *groggy* on returning home, and should be given the same general post-operative care as the female. Consult your own veterinary surgeon on this.

Neutering in the male or female does not produce a fat or sluggish cat. This is a result of over-feeding. With proper care and management the neutered cat should have a long active happy life.

MONORCHIDS AND CRYPTORCHIDS

In male cats either one, or both testicles may be retained in the abdomen. In this case your veterinary surgeon may either advise you to wait for 6 months and then return your cat for another examination, or if the cat is more mature may suggest an abdominal operation, since a cat which has one abdominal testicle will show all the undesirable characteristics of a full tom.

Chapter 4

CARING FOR THE ADULT CAT

Adoption

People become owners of adult cats for two reasons: either they adopt a cat, or almost as frequently a cat adopts them. It seems that cats have an instinct which leads them to homes where they will be welcome. The usual picture is that a rather hungry looking cat is seen hanging about the garden. If it is fed its appearances become more frequent, until almost imperceptibly it becomes established as a regular member of the family. It is sometimes rather hard to determine the reason for this movement in the cat population. Some that are obviously hungry and uncared for may have come from bad homes, or they may be un-neutered toms who have wandered too far away in search of females and become lost. In other cases it seems that they just did not like their original home; perhaps there was a child or a dog who made life difficult for them and they simply moved on to find somewhere more to their liking.

Problem cats

A cat which has had one good home will usually change owners without too much stress providing that conditions are similar. However adopting a cat which has been badly treated, or which has been wandering and fending for itself for sometime can present problems. Even after years of kindness and regular feeding it may still become terrified if it is shut in a room or if it hears a sudden noise or a strange voice.

HOW LONG SHOULD YOU KEEP HIM IN?

It is almost impossible to make a definite rule as to how long a cat should be kept in his new home before it can be considered safe to let him out alone. Much depends on the area and whether there is heavy traffic which may constitute a danger and also on the temperament of the cat; a nervous cat may easily bolt if it is startled and try to return to its original home.

If your cat will wear a harness or a collar and lead (as many Siamese do) it is a good plan to walk him round the new garden under supervision, allowing plenty of time for him to inspect and smell everything, before he is given his first taste of freedom.

UNDERSTAND THE PSYCHOLOGY OF THE CAT

In the normal healthy cat hunger is a strong controlling factor, so when you let your new pet outside alone for the first time see that it is just before a mealtime is due. In this way you can be certain that however interesting the outside world may seem he will be strongly motivated to return home.

Taking care

If you live near a busy road do not make the mistake of thinking that your cat will remain safely in the back garden. They are extremely inquisitive animals and inevitably in time their curiosity will cause them to wander further afield and into danger.

It may be worth considering constructing a wire netting enclosure in the garden to allow your cat a little freedom and fresh air without risk, as we advise for kittens (Chapter 3).

LIVING IN A FLAT

Exercise

A flat is not the ideal place to keep a cat, unless it has some access to the outside, even if it is only over the roofs for exercise purposes. If it is a case of rescuing a stray it is certainly true that a kind home in a flat is better than no home at all but unfortunately if conditions are too restricted cats become bored. It is then that destructive habits such as clawing furniture, or even wallpaper are likely to be a problem.

PUTTING THE CAT OUT

At one time it was accepted practice to put the cat out at night—regardless of the weather—but today on grounds of humanity and in today's heavy traffic, many owners prefer to keep their pets in.

If you feel happier to know that your cat is safely inside at night try to call him in each evening at the same time and reward his return with a few cat biscuits, a piece of cheese or some other treat. This produces what is known as a conditioned reflex which may become so accurate as to make you suspect that your cat has a wrist-watch.

CAT DOORS

Freedom

For cats which persistently come home late, or for those who are always on the wrong side of the door asking to come in, the cat flap may prove to be the answer. This consists of a small flap, just large enough to admit a cat, which is let into one of the lower panels of the house door (these can now be bought pre-fabricated at pet stores and hardware shops). They are certainly of help to owners who have to be away from home for hours at a time and can thus allow their cat some freedom knowing that it will be able to come in if the weather changes. They do have the slight disadvantage that some cats are inclined to invite their less reputable feline friends in as well.

A cat flap let into a door. Make sure it is placed low enough for your cat to step through.

If your cat is reluctant to use the cat flap at first, try leaving it wedged open for a few days until the cat accepts that it is a normal entry route.

Cat shelters
As an alternative to the cat door a cat shelter may be useful for owners who have to be out a lot. This can take the form of a wooden box or crate with a blanket inside and perhaps a plastic cover to make it waterproof in bad weather, placed in a sheltered spot in the garden.

NAME AND ADDRESS

Tag
As soon as your new cat arrives buy him a cat collar and identification tag (see Chapter 3). There is always the risk that an adult cat may try to return to his previous home and this is the first place to enquire if he should be lost, assuming the distance is reasonable.

HEALTH CHECKS FOR THE NEW ARRIVAL

If your new adult cat comes from a friend or a neighbour he will probably be healthy and you will be able to check on any past history of vaccination, neutering or illness. With a genuine stray a health check may present more problems.

THINGS TO LOOK FOR

If your new cat seems listless, ill, or is unable to eat consult a veterinary surgeon as soon as possible. If you are unable to pay the fees of a private veterinary surgeon look out for a clinic run by the PDSA, RSPCA, Blue Cross, or other welfare organisations where you can obtain advice and help either free or at little cost.

'Flu	Sneezing, sore or runny nose and eyes may indicate flu, or a catarrhal infection.
Ears	Shaking the head or scratching the ears, or bare places behind the ears may indicate ear mite infection (see Chapter 5).
Fleas	Poor coat or bare patches in the fur may indicate the presence of fleas or other parasites. A dusting with Sherley's Permethrin Flea Powder or Vamoose Pet Powder should correct this (see Chapter 5) and you can fit a Sherley's Cat Collar to provide continuing protection. If the skin condition does not respond to your first aid measures quite quickly consult a veterinary surgeon who will advise you if other treatment is needed.
Fighting	Un-neutered male cats are often covered with wounds, scratches or even abscesses as a result of fighting (see Chapter 7 for advice on treatment). If your newly adopted tom is to become a family pet it is best to have him neutered or he may wander away again to join the ranks of the homeless cats.
Worms	Cats which have been living wild and eating mice and other rodents are often infected with tapeworm and a routine dosing with a Sherley's worming treatment is a wise precaution (see Chapter 5).

NEUTERING

In the case of a male cat your veterinary surgeon will be able to tell you if it has been neutered if you are unsure but in the case of the female it is not as a rule possible to be certain. In many cases young female cats which are straying are found to be in kitten and the new owner may find that they have suddenly a large family to care for. However since kittens are not always easy to find homes for it is as well to have the newcomer neutered (or spayed) as soon as possible (see Chapter 3).

Vaccination	If your new cat comes from a good home you will probably find that it has been immunised against virus enteritis (see Chapter 3) but it may require booster injections.
	In the case of a stray it is unlikely to have received any protection of this kind and it is best to consult your veterinary surgeon to decide when vaccination should be carried out.

TRAINING A NEW ARRIVAL

Own bed	Establishing a code of behaviour can present problems with an adult cat but it is important if he is to fit in as a member of the new family. For the first week at least it is probably best to keep the cat to one room, preferably the kitchen. Provide him with his own comfortable bed and he will have no excuse for sleeping on yours. If it is placed in a quiet warm spot he will soon settle in and feel at home. If there are dogs or children in the house a raised shelf may allow the newcomer more security and peace of mind. It may be a good idea to pin a notice to the kitchen door saying 'Cat within—please close doors' to remind everyone in the house.
Toilet training	It will almost certainly be necessary to put a litter tray down for the first days (see Chapter 3) and this can present problems at first for an older

cat which has been trained to go out. However if the box or tray is put in a quiet corner of the room and the cat is left undisturbed the situation will usually resolve without too much trouble.

If you do not intend your cat to sit on the chairs you must be firm and persistent about this from the start but try to avoid shouting or frightening him. He may have come from a home where standards were very different and will find it hard to understand new rules and new commands.

BAD HABITS

Unfortunately an adult cat may have acquired bad habits which can be hard to deal with. As far as most owners are concerned scratching or sharpening claws on the furniture are the most serious (see Chapter 3).

Scratching post

See that your cat has as much freedom and exercise outside as possible. Provide him with an indoor scratching post for times when he must stay in. See that the claws are kept reasonably short—but if all these measures prove ineffective simply resolve to see that he is never left unsupervised in any room where damage may be done. If it proves impossible to reform your cat completely at least you can keep damage to a minimum. Claw removal may be considered as a last resort—(see Chapter 3).

Problems

Cats which are dirty in the house present a serious problem. As a species they normally tend to be almost obsessionally clean and modest in their habits, but if as a result of illness, change of home or some emotional stress their training breaks down the situation may be difficult to remedy. Consult your veterinary surgeon to check if there is any physical cause for the behaviour. If this is not the case consider installing a cat door to allow easy access to the outside, see that there is always a clean litter tray available and resign yourself to confining the cat to one room only in the house, where the minimum of damage will result.

Birds

Killing birds, while it cannot strictly be called a bad habit, since it is a normal instinct for cats, can be very upsetting to bird lovers. The most effective way to deal with this is a bell on the collar. After all a civilized well-fed cat is killing purely for pleasure and to prevent this as far as possible is not unreasonable or unkind.

Stealing

Unfortunately even very well-fed cats are inclined to steal if they get the opportunity. See that as far as possible food is not left out to provide temptation but also make a strict rule that your cat is never allowed to jump on to tables or working surfaces. If he attempts to do so clap your hands sharply saying 'No', or smack your hand sharply with a rolled newspaper. This is in the cat's own interest as well since each year many cats suffer burned pads as a result of jumping onto hot electric cooker plates.

FEEDING

Choosey cats

When a stray cat is taken in it is as a rule hungry and will gratefully eat any food that is offered. However there is a natural tendency on the part of the owner to make up for past deprivation by feeding to capacity, with the result that the once hungry cat becomes choosey and starts to refuse foods that it previously enjoyed. In many cases this sets up a cycle in which the owner searches for new and interesting foods which the cat at first enjoys and then as it becomes satiated, rejects. In desperation the owner may buy vitamin pills, or consult a veterinary surgeon to induce the supposedly under-nourished cat to eat.

Normal

Certainly no one would wish that cats should go hungry and this kind of rather obsessional behaviour on the part of cat owners is usually a harmless foible. On the other hand there really is no need to create a faddy and demanding monster out of a perfectly normal cat. It is not even necessary to supply changes in the diet (although all cats enjoy an occasional treat of left-over meat or game in their food). If a good high protein food is supplied in the correct amounts a normal healthy cat will eat and enjoy it every day. Variety does not seem to be a requirement.

If your cat seems listless and rejects his food, or if he has difficulty in chewing or swallowing, you should consult a veterinary surgeon as soon as possible but if your healthy, lively cat starts to reject his meals the answer lies in your own hands. Reduce the amount given at each meal drastically until the appetite returns.

NUTRITIONAL REQUIREMENTS

In the wild state the cat lived entirely on the small rodents or birds that he was able to kill. These supplied not only the protein, fat, vitamins and minerals that he required but also the greater part of the fluid content of the diet.

In the civilized world the cat still has a very high dietary requirement of protein and unlike the dog he is not able to substitute carbohydrate for this to any great extent without losing condition. He also has a higher fat requirement than the dog and fat added to prepared cat foods greatly increases the palatability.

Vitamins and minerals

The normal adult cat will find his needs for vitamins and minerals are supplied adequately in a balanced diet (as suggested below) but for the pregnant or lactating cat (see Chapter 2) or for the growing kitten (see Chapter 3) or following illness, a supplement may be needed.

WHAT TO FEED

Balanced diet

Over the last 10 years there has been an almost revolutionary change in the feeding of cats—mainly for the better. Where previously most cats were fed a diet of meat scraps, lights, or white fish (often deficient in protein and vitamins), nowadays the great proportion are fed on pre-packaged manufactured foods. While these are not necessarily better than good quality fresh meat and fish, they have been carefully formulated to provide a balanced meal for the average cat, they are readily available, easy to store and prepare and probably overall are cheaper than any equivalent food.

FRESH FOODS

Meat

Meat and offal of all kinds can be fed (cooked or raw), although it should be remembered that lights (lungs) are low in protein value and should not be fed as a total diet.

Liver

Liver is rich in Vitamin A (a vitamin that the cat is not able to synthesise and which is essential to health) and makes a good addition to the diet if given once weekly. However some vitamins in excess can cause harm and an exclusive diet of liver can lead to disorders in the bony skeletal system.

Rabbit

Rabbit and game of all kinds are very popular with cats and are ideal for tempting the appetite of a sick cat.

Fish

Fish is a useful food, though if white fish is used as the only food it can lead to vitamin deficiency. It is best prepared in a pressure cooker and the softened bones provide a good source of minerals for the pregnant cat. Canned fish such as pilchards or sardines have a good food value and surprisingly many cats seem to enjoy the tomato sauce as well.

Cheese

Cheese is a good source of protein and is well accepted by most cats. Vegetable protein (soya, etc) can be used only as a partial substitute for animal protein in the diet, which puts cats at a disadvantage in the world where protein is becoming increasingly scarce.

Vegetables

The cat is able to synthesise its own supply of Vitamin C and green vegetables are not necessary in the diet, although as many owners will have noticed some cats like to eat grass, while others have even more exotic tastes and enjoy cucumber and other vegetables without any ill effects.

Bones

Cats enjoy bones to eat almost as much as dogs and since they are more careful and fastidious feeders and do not bolt their food, they suffer much less from the results of swallowing sharp or indigestible fragments. However large fish bones can become wedged in the mouth or throat, so they should be avoided if possible.

Bread

Carbohydrates (bread, non-meat biscuit meal) are not a normal constituent of the cat's diet but small amounts can be added to the food, providing that it also contains an adequate amount of protein.

CANNED FOODS

The canned foods (meat, fish, rabbit etc) which are prepared by the leading manufacturers are carefully and scientifically formulated to supply a total food for a normal cat and they can provide a very satisfactory and trouble-free method of feeding throughout a cat's life. Care of course should be taken, as with any canned food, to see that once it is opened it is not exposed to contamination and it is better if part of a tin has been refrigerated to allow it to return to room temperature before feeding.

SEMI-MOIST

The semi-moist types of food are a recent addition to the cat's menu and they are a more concentrated food. It should be remembered that fresh foods contain over 90% of water, so if a semi-moist food is introduced it is important to see that the cat is receiving sufficient additional fluid in the diet in the form of milk or water. However this type of food seems to be very palatable and well accepted by cats. It is particularly easy to store and feed.

DRY FOODS—CAT BISCUIT

This is a food with a high protein and fat content which most cats enjoy very much. However it is more concentrated and has an even lower fluid content than the semi-moist foods and suffers from the same disadvantages. Since cats were originally desert dwellers they are accustomed to getting their fluid requirements from the solid part of their diet. When the fluid value of the food stuff alters they do not seem to compensate as much as would be expected by drinking, even though water is available. Consequently some opinions have attributed the recent increase in bladder ailments in the cat (feline urethral syndrome—see Chapter 7) to the increased consumption of dry food. For this reason many owners find it more satisfactory to use biscuit as a supplement to canned or fresh food rather than as a total diet.

LIQUIDS

Milk

Milk is an important food for the young kitten and while it is not necessary for the adult cat it is obvious that many of them enjoy it. Fresh milk or Lactol are useful foods in convalescence and for the lactating female with a litter to feed.

Occasionally allergy to cow's milk is seen in some cats and it seems that it may cause digestive disorders especially in Siamese cats. However contrary to the old wive's tale, milk is not a source of roundworms.

Water

Water—although as we have seen many cats drink very little water, it is important to see that it is always available, especially in hot weather, or when feeding a low moisture food.

AMOUNTS TO FEED

General
guide

It is not possible to lay down definite rules on feeding, since even within the species conditions of life and dietary requirements can vary. For instance the young growing cat requires proportionally much more food than the mature adult. However as a general guide, most adult cats require between 5 and 8 ounces daily of a high protein food, according to weight and in practice this works out at ½ a small tin of cat food twice daily for the average to small cat (with milk as well if wanted). The larger cat requires the same amount with the addition of a small quantity of cat biscuit, or household meat or fish scraps if they are available. Remember of course that if your particular cat does not appear to make satisfactory progress it is essential to visit your veterinary surgeon for guidance suited to the individual case.

HOW OFTEN TO FEED

Number of meals   In the wild state the cat would probably have eaten only once in 24 hours but under home conditions most owners find it more satisfactory to divide the meal and feed twice, while for the young kitten or the pregnant cat at least 3 meals daily are necessary (see Chapters 2 and 3).

Food should not be left down all day and in particular biscuits should not be left to be nibbled at will. This is a certain way to ruin the appetite and to produce an obese cat. If a meal is not finished at once it should be picked up and nothing further offered until the next mealtime. Over eating is just as harmful for cats as it is for humans and makes them prematurely old. By giving your cat a well balanced diet without excess you will increase his chances of a long, active and healthy life.

GROOMING

While grooming dogs is accepted as a normal part of ownership there is a tendency for owners to assume that cats need no attention at all. Unfortunately this is far from the truth.

Some short-haired cats do keep themselves very trim, with constant licking and grooming, but during the moulting season even they are unable to cope with the enormous amounts of hair which are either shed on to carpets or furniture or worse still swallowed.

Persian, or long-haired cats on the other hand, require very much more attention and must be regarded as a time-absorbing hobby.

Moulting   In the wild state it is probable that cats had one heavy moult during the hot summer months and then grew a thick new coat for the winter. Today, with the increase in central heating most owners will agree that moulting seems to take place throughout the year.

Regular grooming is essential—for smooth hairs weekly, for long coats three times weekly, or if they are to be kept in show condition, daily.

START OUT THE RIGHT WAY

Choose a suitable place for grooming, if possible a utility room, outhouse, or garage to avoid the nuisance of flying hairs in the house and check that doors and windows are securely shut. Place your cat on a table of comfortable height with a non-slip surface if possible.

The right tools   You will need:—
A fine-toothed, strong steel comb and a brush (a strong nylon hair brush is ideal)
A pair of blunt-ended scissors and nail clippers
A little surgical cotton wool to remove any discharge from eyes and ears
An insecticidal dusting powder such as Sherley's Pet Powder.

Start with the comb first to remove any tangles. Work down from the head, under the chin and behind the ears, then down the back and tail.

Finally turn the cat on his back and groom underneath. Then follow with a brushing to remove the loose and dead hair. In a short-haired cat this is quite a simple process as a rule, but with a long-haired cat and especially in the moulting season if the coat has been neglected, there may be not only tangles but thick felt-like matts, especially behind the ears, at the base of the spine and under the abdomen, which can be extremely difficult to remove. The best method of dealing with this problem is to raise the matted lumps of hair away from the skin gently with the comb and then cut the underlying hair using blunt ended scissors (taking great care not to cut the cat in the process). This will of course, for a while, leave unsightly bare patches, but the hair grows in again very quickly and the comfort and well being of the cat are of much more importance than his appearance.

Matts

Not a one-man job

It need hardly be said that unless the cat is a very placid one this task requires two people, so try to get a friend to help.

Removing severe tangles can prove a very painful for the cat and a very difficult one for the owner. If it really seems insurmountable consult your veterinary surgeon. He may be willing to arrange for your cat to be groomed and *de-matted* under sedation (and then resolve never to allow your pet to get into such a condition again).

WHILE GROOMING:—

Fleas

Check for the signs of fleas (see Chapter 5) and apply an insecticidal dusting powder if necessary.

Mites

Check ears for waxy deposits which may indicate the presence of ear mites (see Chapter 5).

Eyes

Check eyes for any discharge. Tear staining can be a problem on white cats. Cut away any badly stained hair and bathe with sterile (boiled) water or Sherley's Tear Stain Remover.

Teeth

Check the mouth not only for bad teeth which may need attention but also for the heavy tartar deposits which often form around the teeth (see Chapter 7—Teeth). Regular scaling may be necessary in some cases to maintain a healthy mouth but as a rule this is best carried out by a veterinary surgeon and under sedation or general anaesthetic.

Nails

Cats do not as a rule need regular trimming if they have the opportunity to get out and climb trees. However in cases where they are inclined to tear at the furniture it may help to trim just the very tip of the nails with nail clippers. The nail contains a strong nerve and blood supply, so it is important to understand that it is only the dead horny tip that is to be cut. If you feel uncertain about the amount to take off ask your veterinary surgeon or animal welfare clinic to show you.

Tapeworms

The presence of tapeworms may sometimes be detected by the presence of dried-up segments, rather like melon seeds, adhering to the fur in the anal region (see Chapter 5).

BATHING

Cats tend to object to bathing even more than dogs and it is not as a rule necessary to bath them if grooming is carried out regularly, except in the case of show cats, or white cats (see later in this chapter).

Dry

A dry shampoo such as Sherley's Grooming Powder can be useful if it is properly applied. Follow the manufacturer's instructions and be sure to brush the powder completely out of the coat, to leave it clean and shining.

Grooming will not be an ordeal if it is carried out at least weekly. After the more difficult work of brushing and combing take a little time to stroke your cat and tell him how handsome he looks. He will appreciate it.

PREPARING A CAT FOR SHOW

Good condition

The general advice given in this chapter on Cat Care applies to all pets but if a cat is to be entered for shows it is essential that its coat should be kept in good condition all the year round. There can be no question of resorting to scissors to remove tangles; tangles must not be allowed to form. However it is a pity to make a cat a house prisoner simply in the interest of his appearance and many breeders feel that cats which live in centrally heated homes really need the contact with the cold outside world to produce a thick and glossy coat.

For short-haired cats follow the routine suggested earlier in the chapter and simply finish by polishing the coat by smoothing over (in the natural direction of the hair) with a soft duster.

Long-haired cats require more attention and it is essential to be certain that the grooming is thorough and that no knots are left anywhere in the coat. Light-coloured cats may benefit from a bath and this is best carried out 2-3 days before a show.

Shampoo

Use lukewarm water and a reliable veterinary shampoo such as one of the Sherley's range, lathering at least twice. Be sure to rinse very thoroughly (a spray tap fitting is a great help) and see that the cat is kept in a warm even temperature while drying. If the cat is fairly placid use either an electric hairdryer, or better still a heated styling brush to bring up a fluffy coat. In the case of a long-haired cat the final brushing out should be against the natural direction of the coat to produce a really fluffy effect.

Dry shampoos, or simply talcum powder, can be used to prepare the coat but once again it must be emphasised that it is important to remove all powder from the coat, not only for the cosmetic effect but because a cat could be disqualified if traces of powder are seen.

SHOWING AND BREEDING PEDIGREE CATS

There may be some extrovert felines who really enjoy showing off and being admired but the majority would probably say, if they could speak, that the glory of winning at shows hardly compensated for all that they had to endure in washing, brushing and combing beforehand. However there is no doubt that the work of the National Cat Club and the Governing Council of the Cat Fancy in promoting shows has done a great deal for the welfare of cats in general and in increasing interest and concern for them among the general public.

REGISTRATION

There are often small local shows of a general nature where children can enjoy showing their pets but if cats are to be shown at any of the shows run by the NCC or the GCCF they must first be registered (unless they are shown in the Household Pet class).

Cats may have two names:—
a prefix which is the 'family name' or registered name of the breeder and an affix which is the name of the individual cat.

Costs The charge for a prefix registered for the life of the breeder with the GCCF is £20.00.

Prefix holders: £2.00 per kitten or cat.

Non-Prefix holders: £3.00 per kitten or cat.

Information Further information and registration forms may be obtained by sending a stamped, addressed envelope to the Secretary of the GCCF, Mrs W Davis, Dovefields, Petworth Road, Witley, Surrey GU8 5QW. She will also supply the following which will be useful to the prospective cat owner:

show list for current year,
club list,   charge £1.00 each
show rules.

Completed applications and fees should be sent to: The Receptor, GCCF, 28 Brendon Road, Watchet, Somerset, TA23 0AX.

It will be realised that over the years many of the more obvious names have been taken (and they cannot be re-used for 20 years) so it is wise to look for unusual names and to give a choice. Certain categories of names cannot be used and these are defined in the registration certificate application form, so it should be read through thoroughly before completing and returning.

Registration lasts throughout the life of the individual cat but if the cat is sold it cannot be shown until it is transferred to the new owner. The appropriate form can be obtained from the Register of the GCCF and a small charge will be made.

SHOWING

Anyone who is interested in showing or breeding cats would be wise to attend some shows in their own neighbourhood to decide which breed they would like to specialise in and to try to form an idea in their own mind as to what constitutes a good specimen, as this is vital to their future success.

By attending cat shows the prospective owner will have the opportunity not only to acquire a judgement of the points of the show cat but also to meet and talk to breeders.

In this way it may be possible to find the kitten, or kittens that are required but alternatively the local paper will almost certainly carry advertisements from time to time. If you are prepared to go further afield. *Cats*, the official newspaper of the GCCF carries advertisements, offical notices and show reports from all over the country.

However one should never make the mistake of buying a kitten unseen through an advertisement. Apart from the fact that on human and practical grounds pet animals should never be sent by rail unescorted unless it is absolutely unavoidable, the old saying *Buyer Beware* still applies. If your new kitten does not match up to the advertisement or arrives in poor condition, you may find it difficult to obtain redress.

Finding out about shows
The Secretary of the GCCF will supply you with a list of cat shows on receipt of a stamped addressed envelope and a fee of £1.00. A copy of the show rules (£1.00 + sae) is available from the GCCF and anyone wishing to participate in showing would be wise to study them. This also applies to more experienced exhibitors since they are under an obligation to be aware of changes in the rules.

Shows are of two main categories:

Championship Shows—where challenge certificates are awarded. The winner of three of these certificates (awarded at different shows) becomes a champion.

Exemption and Sanction Shows—challenge certificates are not awarded at these shows but they give breeders and especially newcomers to the cat fancy the opportunity to compare their cats with others and judge their potential for future shows.

Cats will of course be entered in their appropriate classes such as 'kittens under 9 months' and at some shows there are classes for neuters.

PREPARING A CAT FOR SHOW

The actual grooming and preparation has already been dealt with earlier in the chapter but it also goes without saying that if a cat is to be shown it must be in the peak of physical condition. There will be a veterinary examination before admittance to the show, and a slight discharge from the eyes, or even the presence of one flea can cause disqualification.

Vaccination
Show cats should be vaccinated against feline enteritis and cat 'flu', but vaccination should not be carried out later than 3 weeks before the show.

Feeding	If the cat is going to the show in the morning it may be given a small meal first thing. A container for water should be provided and a litter tray (peat litter will usually be available). In addition each cat may have one plain white blanket.
Travelling	It is essential to have a strong roomy cat box (see later in Chapter) and also one which can be easily and quickly opened to avoid delays at the veterinary inspection. Your cat should be accustomed in advance to travelling and to spending several hours in a confined space. It is also important that it should be quite used to being handled by strangers, since a cat which cannot be taken out of its cage will be disqualified.

ADMISSION

Admission and 'vetting' usually starts between 9.00 and 10.00 am in the morning, though in some cases cats may be admitted on the previous evening and housed overnight. They must arrive in a proper box and not be brought on lead and harness, or carried in.

Pen

During the show the cat must be confined in its appropriate pen. You will have been given a tally number with your cat on admission and the cage will have the corresponding number.

Cats are not lead, or held for showing as is the case at dog shows. The exhibitor must leave the arena but may sometimes watch from a gallery and the judge will make the rounds. Each cat will be lifted out on to a table and judged in turn. Later the result will be displayed on a board.

Cat shows usually finish at 6.00 pm, but owners are allowed to feed their cats during the afternoon if they wish.

Showing cats cannot be considered a profitable proposition in any way. The cash prizes are usually very small and the time and travel which is involved as well as the entry fees (usually about 70p per cat) leaves the exhibitor well out of pocket. However as a hobby it obviously holds a great fascination for cat lovers and for the serious cat breeder showing adds a prestige and a value to their kittens.

Cat clubs

In most areas there are cat clubs devoted to the various breeds, Siamese, Burmese, Abysinnia, etc. These clubs hold shows locally under the jurisdiction of the National Cat Club. The main large shows of the year, such as the huge NC Club Show at Olympia, are usually held in London.

BREEDING PEDIGREE CATS FOR SHOW AND FOR SALE

Don't go into cat breeding with the idea of making money. It can sometimes be profitable if you have several healthy litters in turn but feeding and veterinary charges, together with the cost of attending shows makes it more likely that you will operate at a loss. It is much safer to regard it as a hobby to be enjoyed for its own sake.

Choose one or if you wish two healthy female kittens, either at 8 weeks, or nearer breeding age at 9 months-1 year but realise that you will have to pay more for an older female (or queen) which appears to 𝗁 potential, or which has already been shown successfully.

Don't make the mistake of buying a male and a female. This causes considerable difficulties once the female commences to come into season if you do not want to breed at once.

KEEPING A STUD CAT

While this may be quite profitable it is not always easy. An unneutered male if it is allowed freedom, will range abroad constantly in search of females and will usually become scarred and battered as a result of fighting. On the other hand, a tom is not an ideal house cat and if it is deliberately kept in may start (especially in the breeding season) to urinate or spray in the home and the resulting smell is both persistent and very unpleasant.

Pen Ideally a stud cat should be kept in an outdoor pen with an exercise area and an inner pen that can be heated. This should be reasonably large so that visiting females can be introduced for mating when necessary.

MATING

As a rule no assistance is needed, although the cats should be supervised to avoid injuries and to be certain that mating has taken place. They may mate several times within the space of a few hours and since ovulation appears to occur as a response to mating, pregnancy usually follows.

In cases where a mating proves unsuccessful the owner of the tom may allow a second mating without charge but this should be ascertained in advance as it is not an invariable rule. In many cases it may be possible to leave a queen for a day or two if she is rather unsettled at first, to be certain of a satisfactory mating.

CARE OF THE FEMALE

Season As we have said in Chapter 2 cats usually start to come into oestrus or season at 7-8 months and if mated at this time will become pregnant. However it is not wise to start breeding intentionally much before one year, to allow the cat to finish growing and reach maturity.

This causes considerable problems. The female in oestrus is quite determined to get out and especially in the case of the Siamese will miaow loudly and persistently. If it should get out it will almost certainly be mated by a neighbouring tom cat and will produce a litter of cross-breds. This will not as some people suppose spoil the cat for future pedigree breeding but it will obviously waste a certain amount of time. However, while cross-bred kittens from Siamese, or other pedigree females do not usually have the typical colouration of the parent, they do inherit many of the breed characteristics and readily find homes as pets as a rule.

It is possible to postpone the onset of oestrus by means of an injection (usually for a period of about 6 months). If the problem of keeping a

...nale confined to the house proves particularly difficult in your in-/vidual circumstances, it is worth discussing the advisability of this ...eatment with your own veterinary surgeon.

...Before the time arrives when you wish to have your cat mated try to ...get in touch with the owner of a suitable stud cat in your area. For information concerning Cats at Stud contact the applicable Breed Club. A list of Affiliated Clubs is available from the GCCF (at the address given) price £1.00 + sae.

Pregnancy The advice given on diet and general care in pregnancy in Chapter 2 applies equally to pedigree cats. However pedigree cats are often more nervous and highly strung and extra care may be required at the time of the birth.

Prepare a cardboard box with a warm (not hot) hotwater bottle covered with a soft blanket. If the mother cat becomes agitated during the birth of the kittens, any that have already arrived can be removed to safety and kept in a warm place, to be returned as soon as she becomes more calm.

Cord In some instances if the mother cat is nervous and upset and does not bite through the umbilical cord it may be necessary for the owner to ligate it (see Chapter 2—Cutting the Cord).

VETERINARY HELP

It may be a wise precaution to advise your own veterinary surgeon of the expected arrival of the kittens and to find out what arrangements he makes for emergency calls after hours if it should become necessary.

REARING AND WEANING THE KITTENS—See Chapter 3

Finally do obtain pedigree forms well in advance and have them made out before advertising the kittens for sale.

TRAVEL AND HOLIDAYS

Alternatives Holiday time presents a problem to the cat owner. The alternatives are as a rule either putting the cat in kennels, or leaving him at home to be cared for by a neighbour. Or there may be a third solution in taking the cat with you. This may sound impractical but cats are becoming more sophisticated today and it is not uncommon to hear of owners who take their cats away with them, even on caravan holidays. However this is a habit which should be started young and it would not be wise to attempt it with a middle aged or nervous cat. If a cat is to travel with you it is important to get him accustomed to wearing a harness or a collar and lead early in life.

LEAVING THE CAT AT HOME

If you have anyone who will stay in the house this is ideal. Cats are very attached to places and if they are left in their own homes and given their usual meals it seems that they do not miss their owners too much. If however the cat is left at home, with a neighbour coming in to feed him, or shut him in at night the situation is less happy. There is always the chance that your pet might become involved in an accident and no-one would know. Alternatively he might become ill and involve the friend or neighbour in unexpected difficulties.

Kennels, or Catteries suffer from two main disadvantages:—
1. Few cats are happy when suddenly removed from home and transferred to a strange environment however well they are treated.
2. There is always risk of infection when a cat which has lived a fairly secluded life is brought in contact with other cats. Cat enteritis and cat 'flu are the main dangers.

CAT ENTERITIS

Most cats are now vaccinated against feline enteritis and providing booster injections are given there is usually a satisfactory level of immunity (see Chapter 2).

CAT 'FLU

Cat 'flu is an ever present danger and the disease itself may vary with the severity of the outbreak, from a mild attack of sneezing to a serious pneumonia, or it may leave a cat with a permanent catarrhal condition. Vaccination against this disease has been introduced and it is best for owners to discuss with their own veterinary surgeon the advisability in their particular circumstances.

Young cats settle better in kennels than older ones, so if it is going to be necessary to leave your pet from time to time, try to establish the habit early and accustom him to the occasional absence from his home.

CHOOSING A KENNEL

Check yourself This can be difficult if you are new to the area. Personal recommendation by another cat owner helps but failing this select a kennel or cattery from the local newspaper, or the yellow pages in the telephone directory. Then well before your holiday is due visit and satisfy yourself that the place is clean, secure and well run. Don't leave things until the last minute when it is too late to change your mind.

THINGS TO LOOK FOR WHEN CHOOSING A CATTERY:—

Cages should be clean, large enough for comfort and well ventilated.

Warmth—heated kennels are essential in winter and owners must be prepared to pay for the extra costs. Cats which are used to living in centrally heated homes suffer considerably if they are put in unheated cages.

Exercise runs—if there is not an exercise run attached to each cage there should be an exercise area where a cat can be put out each day.

There should be someone living on the premises by night as well as by day in case of fire. Above all the proprietor should be a person who really cares about and understands cats. Without this the most modern and efficient cattery will not be a success.

Book well ahead—good kennels may become fully booked in the holiday season.

Licensed   Kennels and catteries are inspected and licensed by the local authorities, so if you really feel that a particular kennels was dirty or gave unsatisfactory care it is worth reporting.

Vaccination certificates may be required, so check with your veterinary surgeon if your cat is due for a booster injection.

Ask if you may take your cat's own bed—it will smell like home and may help him feel less homesick.

Food—ask if your cat may have the food he is used to—or take a supply in for him.

Weight   Don't blame the kennel owner if your cat has lost weight when you collect him. It is most unlikely that he has been short of food but unfortunately some cats fret in kennels and refuse to eat. In these cases it is kinder to make arrangements for the cat to stay in his own home if he has to be left again.

A real cat lover will not enjoy his or her holiday knowing his pet is unhappy.

Transport—always use a strong and reliable cat box or basket when transporting your cat. A frightened cat will often struggle to get out— and nothing could be worse than losing your cat in a strange place.

TYPES OF BASKET

Traditional wicker cat baskets are satisfactory as long as the fastenings remain secure. They have the advantage that they are made of natural fibre and have good ventilation but they are difficult to disinfect if it should be necessary following an infectious illness.

Ventilation   Fibre-glass boxes are strong and can be washed out easily and disinfected but it is important to be certain that the ventilation holes are adequate, especially for larger cats, if they are to be kept in them for any length of time.

Wire mesh or metal cages are strong and provide ample ventilation but because they are so open they provide no sense of security to the cat if a strange person (or a strange dog) should approach.

For those cats which travel infrequently, or for short journeys the cardboard cat boxes sold by the various welfare organisations are useful. But be warned, they will not hold a large and frightened cat.

TRAVEL BY SEA, RAIL, AIR

If possible travel with your pet. In a train you will as a rule be allowed to keep a cat in the carriage providing he is in a proper cat box or basket.

It is a sensible plan to line the base of the basket with a sheet of polythene, covered by several layers of newspaper, in case of unexpected accidents.

TRAVELLING UNACCOMPANIED

Strong box

If it is absolutely necessary to send a cat by train unaccompanied, choose a passenger train and notify the recipient to be on the platform to meet it. Use a strong wooden box, which is secure but with adequate ventilation. Line the box with several layers of newspaper and add a blanket for comfort and warmth. See that the box is marked 'Live Cat' or 'Kitten' and that the address of the sender and the recipient are quite clearly visible. Unfortunately even with the most careful arrangements delays and misdirections occur but in this way you can be told whether the cat has reached his destination safely. If you have to send a cat by train unaccompanied, it would be best to contact your local Station Master and clarify the position.

Car

Although the first car journey may prove rather alarming, many cats become quite seasoned car travellers. However it is probably safer for the driver that they should be confined to a basket during the journey.

Sea or air

If it is necessary to send a cat unaccompanied by sea or air it is best to consult one of the firms which specialise in this work (Spratts, or LEP for instance). They will be able to provide a secure and suitable box and will advise you of the regulations governing travel.

WHEN TAKING YOUR CAT ABROAD

Quarantine

When taking your cat out of the United Kingdom you will require a certificate of health given by a veterinary surgeon a few days before leaving. In addition, some countries require your cat to be vaccinated against rabies. In some countries there is a short quarantine period on arrival but because the United Kingdom is free from rabies most places will admit British cats at once. It really is important to find out all these details about the country concerned as soon as possible. Failure to do this may involve you in considerable delay, or heartbreak, if you find that you are unable to take your pet with you.

QUARANTINE REGULATIONS

Rabies

All cats entering either the United Kingdom or Ireland are required to undergo 6 months isolation in a quarantine kennel. This may sound harsh, but it is an essential precaution to prevent the introduction of rabies into this country. Rabies is not only a dreadful disease of animals but the bite from a rabid animal causes a terrible and fatal disease in man. The period between the original infection and the development of symptoms of the disease may be as long as 6 months and this is why the quarantine must be so long. The United Kingdom and Ireland are free from rabies as a result of these very strict regulations but remember if you ever feel tempted to smuggle a cat into the country you are not only breaking the law and risking a heavy fine, but you may be responsible for causing an outbreak of rabies which could cost not only the lives of many pets but many people and wild animals as well.

Government controls The importation of dogs and cats into Great Britain from abroad is controlled by the Ministry of Agriculture, Fisheries and Food, Government Buildings, Hook Rise South, Tolworth, Surbiton, Surrey, or in Scotland, by the Department of Agriculture and Fisheries for Scotland, Chesser House, 500 Gorgie Road, Edinburgh EH11 3AW. No cats may be landed unless a licence is previously obtained for them. All such licences require the animals to undergo detention and isolation for six months on Government Authorised Quarantine Premises and to be twice vaccinated after arrival there with an approved anti-rabies vaccine. Imported cats must be conveyed from the port of entry to the place of detention by authorised Carrying Agents. A list of Carrying Agents can be obtained from the Ministry.

Similar conditions are imposed by the Authorities concerned in Eire, Northern Ireland and the Channel Islands, whilst cats imported from abroad may not enter the Isle of Man until they have completed the requisite six months quarantine in Great Britain, in Eire, or in Northern Ireland.

Provided that they are not actually subject to quarantine restrictions owing to their recent importation from abroad, cats may be moved freely between and within Great Britain, Northern Ireland, Eire, the Channel Islands and the Isle of Man.

CARING FOR THE ELDERLY CAT

With better feeding and medical care the family cat is becoming very long lived. Ages of 16 and 17 years are by no means uncommon and with very little extra care and attention old age can be a very pleasant and contented time.

Feeding Proprietary canned cat foods may still be given and they are particularly suitable for those elderly cats who have lost some, or all their teeth. However elderly appetites can be capricious and the time for indulgence has arrived, so it may be advisable to try fresh foods such as rabbit, fish or mince from time to time to maintain a high protein level and add interest to the diet.

Diets In cases where a specific illness has been diagnosed (such as kidney disease) your own veterinary surgeon will advise you as to the foods which are most suitable for your pet.

Warmth Adequate rest and warm surroundings are of great importance in the case of the elderly cat. In winter particularly old cats may seem to sleep for almost all of the 24 hours, if they can find a cosy place in an airing cupboard, or near a radiator and in summer they select the sunniest spots in the garden for dozing. However in spite of this they will suddenly surprise you by playing like a kitten with a toy or a piece of string.

Medical care A regular visit to your veterinary surgeon or Animal Welfare Clinic (perhaps once a year, or every 6 months) is a wise precaution to be certain that your pet is still well enough to enjoy life.

TROUBLES OF OLD AGE

Teeth Teeth can be a common cause of discomfort and loss of appetite. If your veterinary surgeon advises extractions you will find as a rule that it produces a great improvement in general well being. Hard healthy gums are of much more use for eating than bad teeth.

Nails As the joints become stiffer, cats may be unable to sharpen their own claws and may have difficulty in retracting them when they become caught in cloth. Regular trimming of the overgrown tips of the nails will help to minimise this problem.

Constipation Some elderly cats suffer from a severe type of constipation, largely as a result of loss of muscle tone in the bowel, although it may also be due to the lack of proper exercise, or to swallowing large quantities of hair in the moulting season.

Including liver in the diet (raw or cooked) once or twice weekly will usually have a natural laxative effect. Sherley's Lik-A-Med Laxative is readily taken and suitable for simple constipation.

If these first-aid measures prove ineffective it is best to consult a veterinary surgeon for further advice.

Incontinence Unfortunately many elderly cats lose control of bladder and bowels and however much you love your pet this can make life very difficult. It is of course useless and unkind to blame the animals; this is something they cannot help. Consult your veterinary surgeon who will tell you if any medical help can be given, or if you can expect any improvement in the condition.

EUTHANASIA

In cases where a cat is suffering from a painful and incurable condition, or when your veterinary surgeon advises that life cannot be prolonged with kindness, euthanasia should be considered (see Chapter 7).

Chapter 5

INTERNAL AND EXTERNAL PARASITES

INTERNAL PARASITES

WORMS

It sometimes comes as a shock to an owner to discover that his much-loved pet is the host to quite a number of parasites and the sight of a flea, or worse still a tapeworm segment in an otherwise spotless home can be disturbing. However modern preventative measures for these pests are simple and effective and with reasonable care parasites should not be a problem.

THE RISK TO YOUR PET

The major internal parasites of the cat in this country are not blood suckers but feed on microscopic particles of semi-digested food within the gut. In spite of this, large numbers of the parasites in the stomach, or the lumen of the bowel can interfere with digestion and lead to poor condition in the adult, while in the young kitten the presence of worms and their larval forms in the body can constitute a real danger to life.

ROUNDWORMS
TOXASCARIS AND TOXOCARA

Appearance

Similar to a thin garden worm, these may be up to several inches in length and are sometimes coiled up in a mass. Their colour is whitish, or pinkish brown, owing to ingested food material.

Recognition

The adult worms are passed in the faeces but because of cats' clean habits the worms are not as easily detected in cats as in dogs. They may be vomited and it is not uncommon for an adult cat to expel a single large worm when regurgitating hair.

Symptoms

In the adult cat, few adult worms are found as a rule. The roundworms form a larval stage and then tend to become encysted in the muscle, where in the male, as a rule, they cause no trouble. However in the female under

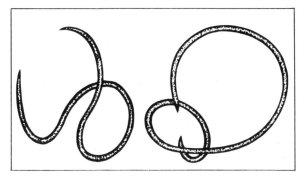

Roundworms.

the influence of hormones during pregnancy, the larvae become active and develop into mature worms which lead to pre- and post-natal infection of the kittens. For this reason the mother cat should be treated for roundworm immediately before kittening and while feeding the litter.

Danger to very young

Young kittens may show quite severe symptoms of poor growth, loss of appetite and abdominal distention as a result of adult worms in the stomach. They may also suffer from the presence of the larval form of the worm which migrates through the liver and the lungs.

Do not dose sick cat

While a kitten affected by heavy roundworm infestation may show the symptoms described above it is a mistake for an owner to assume that worms are the cause of all illnesses in young kittens. Similar symptoms might well indicate the onset of a virus disease and while modern worm remedies are very safe for the normal cat they should not be given to a cat that seems unwell unless the diagnosis is certain or without first checking with a veterinary surgeon or an Animal Welfare Clinic.

How they spread

The life cycle of the roundworm is fairly simple, being transmitted directly from cat to cat. The adult worms are found living freely in the stomach and small intestine where they feed on the partly digested food. When they are mature they shed many thousands of tiny eggs, invisible to the naked eye, which are passed with the faeces and then quickly swallowed again by the cat in grooming, or by the mother cat in cleaning her kittens. The swallowed egg hatches in the stomach to produce a microscopic larva. In the adult animal this larva travels by the blood stream to become enclosed in a cyst in the muscle causing little harm but in the kitten, or the pregnant cat it migrates through the liver and the lungs, where it is coughed up and swallowed, growing to a mature worm in the stomach and repeating the cycle.

Treatment

Starving is not necessary nowadays. Modern worm treatments are not in any way distressing to the patient and they are safe and effective in the normal healthy cat. Sherley's produce a complete range of treatments for roundworm, including tablets, liquid and cream.

Administration

Tablets (which can be finely powdered between two sheets of paper) or liquid medicine can usually be given mixed with the food. However a

67

very slight knowledge of cat psychology will tell you that many cats are extremely suspicious of anything unusual in their meal. This can best be overcome by mixing the medicine with a favourite and strongly flavoured food and by making certain that the cat is really hungry beforehand.

If your cat is really resistant to any foreign substance in the food, administer the medicine on its own following a small meal (see Chapter 6 for advice on this).

Dosing more than once

From the story of the life cycle of the worm you will understand that treatments will only reach the fully developed worms which are in the stomach and for this reason it is necessary to repeat the dosing weekly to be certain of catching the new batch of worms as they develop. This is why a cat that has been treated once for worms without any apparent result may start to pass worms again. It is not that the treatment was ineffective but that a new batch of worms has completed its development.

Risk to man

Much has been written during recent years of the risk of passing worm infection from pets to man and while this should not be minimised or overlooked it should be kept in perspective. Cat tapeworm have (very rarely) been found in man but this is an unlikely risk since the tapeworm is transmitted through an intermediate host (the flea) and it is only by swallowing an infected flea that man could acquire the worm.

Visceral larval migrans

Roundworms however have been implicated in causing a serious (but fortunately rare) condition (visceral larval migrans) in children who have become infected with the migrating cysts of the worm as a result of swallowing the eggs. Fortunately cats appear at present to be considered less of a risk in this respect than dogs possibly because of their cleaner and tidier habits. They do not as a rule defaecate on lawns and public parks where children play. A conscientious owner might consider that it is better to train a cat to use a litter tray all the time to minimise the risk of contamination to the garden if there are children in the family.

Provided that sensible hygienic measures are observed the risk to health of keeping a cat compares very well with many other risks which we accept in life (like crossing roads)—and besides that a cat adds a great deal of affection and companionship to a home.

TAPEWORM
TAENIA AND DIPYLIDIUM SPECIES

Mostly in adults

Tapeworm are more commonly found as parasites of the adult cat rather than the young kitten. The reason for this is not known but it may well relate to the fact that the tapeworm is spread mainly by the flea (the intermediate host) and so it is only as the kitten becomes older and starts to groom itself regularly that it becomes adept at catching (and swallowing) fleas. It may also be true to say that because their tiny front teeth are well adapted to this work cats suffer from tapeworm more frequently than dogs.

What we usually speak of as a tapeworm is actually a series of individual and independent segments (capable of existing on their own) which are linked together, rather like a train and which terminate at the narrow end in a sharp hook (the scolex) which is attached to the lining of the intestine. This hook is often mistakenly spoken of as the 'head' of the worm. The worm may be 2-3 feet in length, yellowish white in appearance and it is not unusual for a cat to harbour several at one time.

The presence of the worm is usually recognised when the mature segments start to be shed via the rectum, or with the faeces, or occasionally when the cat vomits a complete worm. The individual segments are about 1/8″ in length, oval in shape and when they are shed they are alive and capable of some movement. Because of their appearance owners sometimes mistakenly assume that they are roundworms. It is only the complete worm that has the typical 'tape' appearance that gives it its name. To treat your cat effectively it is wise to identify the type of parasite, and the roundworm and the tapeworm are in fact very dissimilar.

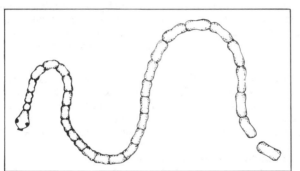

Tapeworm showing the head on the left.

The dried-up segments may also be found sticking to the hair in the anal region and resemble melon seeds.

The actual amount of food that is consumed by tapeworms is so small as to be of no consequence and it is only when the worms are present in large quantities that they may interfere with normal digestion. If your cat starts to lose weight never assume that worms are the cause without first checking with your veterinary surgeon or local animal welfare clinic. However the presence of worms almost certainly causes some discomfort or irritation to the cat and the shedding of segments in the house is aesthetically very unpleasant. If you have definite proof of the presence of worms you should carry out treatment to eliminate these parasites for the good of all concerned.

Tapeworm are never spread directly from cat to cat but require an intermediate host to complete their complicated life cycle. These may be mice or rabbits, but most commonly and especially in the urban family pet the flea is the main vector.

When the mature segments of the tapeworm are passed by the cat they contain many thousands of microscopically tiny eggs. The segments dry out and rupture, liberating the eggs either into the animal's hair or the bedding where they are swallowed by fleas, or into the soil where they eventually find their way into one of the other vectors (rabbits or mice). Within the intermediate host the eggs of the worm hatch out to form a larva, and when the mouse or the flea is eaten by a cat the cycle is completed and the larva develops into a new tapeworm in the gut of its new host.

Control of intermediate host

As you will see, in the case of the tapeworm, eliminating the mature worm is only half the battle. It is necessary where possible to eliminate as well, the intermediate host which provides a constant source of reinfection.

Hunting cats

Many cats are inveterate hunters and in country areas they may quite regularly kill and eat young rabbits. They also kill mice and we are usually quite glad to let them do so. In this situation it is best to carry out a routine of regular treatment with a safe tapeworm remedy.

Fleas

In the case of the family pet cat, fleas are by far the most common source of infection. The regular use of Sherley's Permethrin Powder or Pet Powder and a Sherley's Insecticidal Collar or Band will do a great deal to reduce the nuisance of both fleas and tapeworm (see later section on External Parasites).

Treatment

Tapeworm can prove rather difficult to treat because if the complete worm is not shed, including the scolex or hook, regrowth will recommence very quickly. It is important to use a reliable treatment like Sherley's Tapeworm Tablets and of course to be certain that the cat has swallowed it (see Chapter 6 on administration of medicines).

If worm segments are seen almost immediately after dosing it is probable that your treatment has been ineffective, but if there is a delay of a few weeks reinfection is usually the cause.

Lung worm

The lung worm (Aleurostrongylus) causes respiratory symptoms and pneumonia but it is uncommon and not readily diagnosed by an owner.

Hookworm

This is a true blood sucking worm (Uncinaria) and if present in large quantities can lead to debility and anaemia. Fortunately it is more common in warmer climates and rarely causes trouble in the domestic pet in this country. The worm is very tiny (about ½" long) and is not readily recognised. If you suspect that your cat may be infected it is best to consult a veterinary surgeon for a definite diagnosis.

THE EXTERNAL PARASITES OF THE CAT

FLEAS AND MITES

It should be realised that most household pets unless they receive regular care, will harbour quite a number of external parasites. This is even more true of the cat than the dog, since most cats lead, to some extent, a life of independence and adventure. They are able to cross garden walls at will and hence have more unrestricted contact with others of their species. Fortunately very few of these parasites are of any danger to humans but they do result in considerable loss of condition and of enjoyment of life in the severely affected animal.

THE CAT FLEA

Incidence
The cat flea is the main 'nuisance' parasite of the family cat. Fleas are very active and widespread, especially in the warm, late summer and autumn months. In former times the incidence of infestation decreased sharply with the advent of cold weather, when the fleas tended to retreat into upholstery, or into the crevices of old buildings where they could remain alive but dormant (without food) for several months. Nowadays however, as a result of central heating, our homes are much warmer and fleas have become a year-round, rather than a seasonal, pest.

Transmission to man
The human and the cat flea are distinct and separate species and while humans may occasionally be bitten by cat fleas, the risk is slight.

Appearance
Fleas are blackish brown and shiny in appearance and about 1/16″ in length. They live on the animal's body where they inflict bites with their sharp mouth parts and live on the resulting blood. They do not remain attached to the skin of the animal as do lice but are often found in clusters on the skin, in parts of the body which are not easily reached by the cat in grooming, such as the base of the tail, or behind the ears. They tend to run about the body very rapidly if disturbed (rather than jumping) and they may be quite difficult to find.

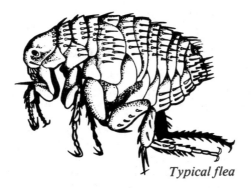

Typical flea

Fleas are most often detected by the presence of the greyish-black, ashlike droppings (often mistakenly thought of as eggs) which can be seen either in the cat's fur, or in its bedding.

Life history
The flea spends much of its life on the body of its host but its microscopic eggs are laid in the animal's bedding, where they hatch out to form larvae which finally turn into adult fleas. It will be understood from this that it is important that the bedding should be kept scrupulously clean

and it is obviously best that cats should not get into the habit of sleeping in armchairs or on beds.

If fleas are a problem it is a good idea to use a simple cardboard box for your cat's bed, together with old pieces of blanket, so that all the bedding can be burnt and replaced weekly.

Symptoms
: The main symptoms of flea infestation are scratching, biting at the fur, or persistent and excessive grooming, or twitching of the back muscles. The presence of fleas causes considerable irritation and distress to the cat and they should not be ignored or accepted as normal.

Flea eczema
: Severe infestation can lead, as a result of the cat's constant biting, or licking with its rough tongue, to a condition known as flea eczema, in which there may be loss of hair, bare patches and even bleeding. Eliminating the fleas will produce an immediate improvement but in severe cases it may be necessary to consult a veterinary surgeon for treatment of the related symptoms.

Young kittens are very susceptible to fleas and it is a good idea to dust any new kitten with an insecticidal powder as a precaution, especially if it comes from a cat's home or pet shop where there was more chance of contact with other cats.

Transmission
: Fleas are also of importance since they provide the major intermediate host of the tapeworm (see earlier section on internal parasites).

Treatment
: Fleas can be treated effectively with insecticidal powders but care should be taken to select one which is intended specifically for cats like Sherley's Permethrin Flea Powder or Pet Powder. It is important to apply the powder thoroughly throughout the coat and then after allowing time for it to act, to brush and comb out the dead or stunned fleas.

Repeat treatment
: The treatment must be repeated at intervals to catch any new developing flea grubs or larvae.

Grooming
: Remember that all cats need regular grooming and control of fleas is much more difficult in a cat which has a matted and neglected coat.

Prevention— the flea collar
: The development of the insecticidal flea collar has made the control of fleas much simpler and more effective. The collar is impregnated with a chemical substance which provides a continuous insecticidal effect over a period of time, killing fleas, lice and other parasites. Provided that it is used strictly in accordance with the manufacturer's instructions, and is renewed when necessary, the collar can be a most effective answer to the flea problem. Sherley's produce both Cat Collars and the longer lasting Flea Bands.

HEDGEHOG FLEAS

Hedgehog fleas are not (as their name implies) a natural parasite of the cat but they can be an occasional nuisance. They are smaller and darker than the cat flea, and are most often noticed clustered in large numbers along the edge of the cat's ears after it has been out in the garden. They may cause some irritation for a while but they can be treated with the powders which are effective against cat fleas, or they will in most cases be found to have disappeared spontaneously in about 24 hours.

LICE

Lice are a much less common parasite of the cat and they are most often seen in cats that are in poor condition as a result of straying, or in unneutered toms which are inclined to wander away and sleep in old buildings.

Recognition   Lice are tiny, pinkish-white in colour and rather spherical in shape. They are slow moving and attach themselves to the cat's skin where they suck blood. They are often most easily identified by the presence of the eggs or 'nits' as they are called. These have rather the appearance of scurf in the coat but examination with a magnifying glass will show whitish shiny seed-like structures which are adhering tightly to each individual hair.

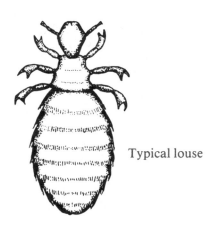

Typical louse

Symptoms   Like those of flea infestation—they include persistent scratching and biting with the formation of bare, or sore areas on the skin.

Treatment   Treatment should be carried out as for fleas but it is important to continue treatment for a period to catch the developing lice as they hatch out from the eggs, since most powders are only effective against the adult form.

Lice also act as intermediate hosts to the tapeworm.

Prevention   **Sherley's Insecticidal Collars are also effective against lice and form the best method of prevention.**

TICKS (SHEEP TICKS)

Ticks are not a normal parasite of the cat, but they are sometimes encountered in moorland areas.

Ticks are also sometimes found on hedgehogs, and this may be a source of infection in towns.

Recognition Ticks are bluish black in colour and rather like a small bean in appearance. They vary in size but after feeding on the host they become engorged with blood and may be up to ½" in size. At this stage they are sometimes mistaken for skin cysts but examination under a magnifying glass will reveal the presence of legs and biting mouthparts near the cat's skin.

Treatment When individual ticks are found they can be removed with tweezers after first soaking with surgical spirit to cause the withdrawal of the biting head. If the head is broken off it may result in a septic wound and in any case it is wise to swab the area with an antiseptic lotion after removal.

However ticks will drop off on their own accord within a day or two and will then remain dormant on the ground until they are picked up by a new host.

Prevention Insecticidal Collars are effective against ticks and they are a sensible precaution in areas where they occur commonly.

Common tick.

HARVEST MITES OR HARVEST BUGS (TROMBICULAR AUTUMNALES)

Harvest mites cause irritation and annoyance to pets (and to humans) in the late summer months. They are of microscopic size, though groups of them may sometimes be seen on the animal's skin as yellowish pin point spots. They cause irritation by burrowing under the skin but the period of infection is brief and they can readily be treated with the same preventative and curative measures as the other skin parasites.

THE RABBIT MITE (CHEYLETIELLA)

This is not easy to diagnose. It is sometimes noticed as a whitish scurf on the coat and may cause skin irritation. Treatment with anti-parasitic powders is effective.

THE EAR MITE (OTODECTES)

The ear mite is one of the most troublesome external parasites of the cat. It is found living exclusively inside the ear canal, a place which even the most determined cat is unable to reach in grooming. It is almost invisible to the naked eye but may readily be seen with a magnifying glass. Large numbers of the mites give a greyish crusty appearance to the inside of the ear. They are not blood suckers but live on particles of wax or exudate.

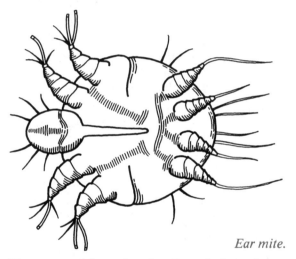

Ear mite.

Recognition
Young cats pick up the mites from their mothers and are often severely infected. The presence of the mites in the ear causes extreme irritation and as a result excessive amounts of wax are formed which cause concrete-like encrustations in the ear. The constant scratching of the kitten causes exudation in the ear and bacterial infection may follow. In severe cases there may be infection of the middle ear and a generalised illness with loss of balance. In these cases it is important to consult a veterinary surgeon or Animal Welfare Clinic for treatment.

In older cats the first symptom to be noticed is often a bare or bleeding patch on the back of the ear. This is caused as a result of the cat's continuous scratching to try to get at the source of the irritation. Unfortunately it is sometimes mistaken for the results of a cat fight by owners who treat the wound on the outside of the ear (with little success) without realising that the cause lies within.

Transmission
Ear mites are not infectious to humans but they are very easily transmitted to other cats or to dogs.

If the diagnosis is certain relief can quickly be obtained by the application of ear drops designed to destroy the mite. Sherley's Canker Lotion Capsules are an effective remedy. Treatment should be repeated at weekly intervals, to catch the new mites as they emerge from the eggs. However if bacterial infection is present (indicated by presence of a bloodstained discharge in the ear) a veterinary surgeon should be consulted.

Where there are severe encrustations of wax within the ear it may be necessary first to cleanse the ear canal before applying ear drops. To do this pour a few drops of olive oil or liquid paraffin into the ear; massage gently from the outside then wipe away oil and wax together with swabs of cotton wool. It is not wise or necessary to use tweezers or any other sharp instrument to clean the ears, since a sudden movement from the cat may result in injury to the sensitive lining of the ear canal.

Any sore places on the back of the ear should be dabbed with an antiseptic lotion but they will heal very rapidly once the source of irritation is removed.

Ear mite infection is an extremely irritating condition. As soon as the cat's ear is touched it will trigger off an intense scratch reflex, which may well result in the owner's hand being lacerated.

For your own protection, before attempting any treatment, swathe the cat completely in a thick towel, or old coat, right up to the neck so that the feet are immobilised (see Chapter 6).

MANGE

The expression 'a mangey cat' is sometimes heard but in fact mange (Sarcoptic or demodectic) is hardly ever seen in the cat. The condition recognised by owners as mange is as a rule eczema (a non-infectious skin condition usually allergic in nature—see list of common ailments in Chapter 7).

The diagnosis of mange is made by demonstrating the presence of mites in a scraping taken from the superficial layers of the skin. If you suspect that your cat may have mange consult a veterinary surgeon.

NOTOEDRIC MANGE

This is again rarely seen. It affects the face and head of the cat and the irritation from the presence of the mite leads to self-inflicted bare or crusty areas. For treatment it is best to consult a veterinary surgeon.

RINGWORM

The extremely contagious skin condition known as ringworm is actually caused by a fungus which invades the individual hairs, causing them to break, or to die and fall out.

Recognition	The typical ringworm lesion is a circular bare place with a crusty surrounding area, which gradually increases in size, surrounded by broken hairs. However any small bare patch, where there is loss of hair without any marked sign of soreness or irritation should be considered suspect and it seems that in some cases cats may be carriers of ringworm without showing any obvious lesions at all.
Transmission	It cannot be too strongly stressed that ringworm is extremely contagious not only to other animals but also to man and more especially to children, partly because their skin is more delicate but also because they spend more time in close contact with pets.
	Cats probably pick up the infection most often from rats and mice but ringworm spores can remain active on woodwork or material for a very long time.
Diagnosis	Always consult a veterinary surgeon at once if you suspect ringworm. He will be able to make a diagnosis by examining the cat under a Wood's glass (which causes the affected areas to fluoresce or glow), or by the microscopic examination of hairs.
Treatment	Treatment is unfortunately very prolonged and recurrence is common. There is now an oral treatment which is effective but the risk of infection to children during the period of treatment and the difficulty of effectively cleansing the home is so great that in severe cases it may unfortunately be considered best to have the cat humanely destroyed.

MAGGOTS

These are not a true parasite of the cat but cats, like other animals, may sometimes be affected by them.

Maggots are produced from the eggs of the common blowfly—just as meat is sometimes affected in summer.

Recognition	The eggs are laid on an infected wound, or on soiled hair and it will be understood that they are usually found on a cat which is already ill and weak (since healthy cats will not allow flies near them). They are most often seen on cats which have been injured and wandered away, especially during the summer months when flies are common.
	This condition is extremely serious. The maggots feed on the cat's flesh and produce a toxic condition which is rapidly fatal.
Treatment	Consult a veterinary surgeon as soon as possible but in the meantime cut away as much hair as possible from the area (it will probably be found to contain more of the tiny yellow eggs). Remove as many maggots as possible with tweezers and swab the area with a mild antiseptic lotion.

Chapter 6

TREATMENT AND FIRST AID IN ILLNESS

Is he ill or not?

Sensible care and proper feeding will do a great deal to keep your cat fit, healthy and active but accidents and illnesses can still occur and it is important to know how to recognise the symptoms of ill health, how to deal with accidents and injuries, and to know when it is necessary to consult a veterinary surgeon.

It is true that cats are not always as easy to deal with as dogs but the average family cat is not a wild tiger and should not be treated as if he is. If the administration of tablets, or liquid medicines, or the treatment of wounds is approached in the right way it should not present problems. It is worth remembering that a cat which is cared for, handled and groomed when he is well will accept medical care much more readily when it becomes necessary.

HOW TO EXAMINE YOUR CAT

Some of this advice may sound obvious but it is surprising how often people overlook the simple rules of common sense and involve themselves in unnecessary difficulties. If your cat is placid and well behaved the advice may well be quite superfluous for you but if you know that your own pet is nervous, or have never tried to examine him before, it is best to take all necessary precautions.

Secure room

Try to choose a room with a good natural or artificial light and check that doors and windows are securely fastened. Your cat may not wish to be examined and will make plans to leave as soon as he suspects your intentions.

Try to choose a reasonably small room and one which is free from places where a cat can hide and not be retrieved easily (the spaces under cupboards and wardrobes for instance). If necessary block these exits off. Hours can be wasted in trying to coax a cross cat out of its retreat. If possible place the cat on a table. It is not easy to make an examination while crawling about on the floor.

Restraint Immobilise the patient as far as possible. This is best done by placing him (or her) in the centre of a really thick blanket or old coat and wrapping it completely around, leaving only the head out, if the head or mouth is to be examined, or leaving space to look at an injury on a limb, or leaving the tail free if the temperature is to be taken. Cats, if they are frightened or in pain, or if they resent treatment will not hesitate to use their sharp claws and teeth to help them escape, so be warned that a small or thin blanket will not be sufficient.

Gloves Some people may prefer to put on a thick pair of gardening gloves as a precautionary measure but these are rarely proof against bites and have the disadvantage of being rather clumsy when handling the cat.

Opening the mouth Wrap the cat up as described above. If possible get a friend to help by standing behind the cat, and holding firmly onto the blanket, restrain him from attempting to raise the front paws. Then place one hand firmly over the cat's head from behind, gripping at each side of the upper jaw and gently tip the head back to open the jaws. This may be sufficient to give a view of the inside of the mouth but it may also help to place the fore finger of the other hand on the point of the lower jaw to depress it slightly at the same time.

ADMINISTRATION OF TABLETS

Smooth-coated tablets usually present little problem. Open the mouth as described above and then drop the tablet at the back of the cat's tongue (as centrally as possible) and quickly shut the mouth, allowing him to swallow.

Rough-coated tablets are inclined to stick and if they are bitter or unpleasant to taste the cat will fight against being given them again. This can be overcome by putting the tablet inside a piece of firm butter (or cheese can sometimes be used) and administering it in the same way.

While some modern medicines are almost tasteless and can be administered in food there are still the exceptions. Even very hungry cats will as a rule examine their food before eating it and they are very quick to discover when any extraneous substances have been added.

LIQUID MEDICINES

These can be dealt with in very much the same way but to avoid spills it is best to put the measured dose in a small bottle, or in an eye dropper. Wrap the cat up completely as before and open the mouth, tipping the head back slightly. Then trickle the liquid on to the cat's tongue and you will find that in most cases it will swallow quite readily and without struggling.

RECOGNISING THE SYMPTOMS OF ILLNESS

Listlessness, disinclination to take food, and a raised body temperature are the main signs of a generalised illness or infection.

Listlessness Healthy cats will often sleep for hours and hours at a time and this is quite normal and typical of carnivore behaviour. However an observant owner will readily detect the differences in the behaviour of a sick cat. It will remain in its own box, or a quiet corner and will show no interest in its surroundings. It will not play, or react to its owner's voice and it will not wash, or stretch itself and rub affectionately against people's legs in the manner which is so typical of the cat which feels well.

Loss of appetite There are two main reasons for apparent loss of appetite. The cat may be unable to eat or it may feel ill and have no interest in eating.

Unable to eat In the first case there is some physical reason why the cat cannot take its food. Typically, it will approach the plate eagerly and then turn away. This may indicate such conditions as a sore mouth resulting from an infection, tooth troubles in the teething kitten, or bad teeth or tooth abscess in the older cat.

It may also be due to a foreign body in the mouth such as a bone lodged across the roof of the mouth, or at the side of the molar teeth. In the case of a bone which is stuck in the throat the cat will often attempt to eat and then will immediately regurgitate food back again.

Unwilling to eat In this case the cat is feeling ill or nauseated and shows no interest when food is offered, or simply turns the head away.

FIRST ELIMINATE OBVIOUS CAUSES

If your cat is a bird killer look for the telltale signs of feathers in the garden, or the over-distended stomach. This type of inappetence usually corrects itself quite quickly but if your cat has not recovered his appetite in 24 hours it may be best to consult a veterinary surgeon.

If you can see no apparent reason for your cat's behaviour although he appears perfectly well and active, it is sensible to allow 24 hours to elapse before taking further advice, but keep him under observation and do not offer alternative or tempting foods. It may well be that your pet has found something unwholesome to eat in a neighbour's rubbish bin and in this case starvation is the best policy.

However if your cat refuses food and at the same time seems listless and quiet, he is probably ill. You should consult a veterinary surgeon as soon as possible.

Temperature The temperature of the cat and other animals is usually taken in the rectum. The normal temperature of a healthy cat is 101.5°F and a rise of even 1° may be a significant indication of illness.

Taking the temperature	Most cats resent having their temperatures taken, so it is best to immobilise the patient in the manner described earlier by wrapping it in a thick blanket. If possible get a friend to help but if this is not possible wrap the cat up, tuck it under one arm, or put it on a table and lean on it while holding onto the tail.
	A heavy bulb veterinary thermometer is easier to read and is slightly less easy to break. First shake the thermometer well so that the mercury falls in the tube. Lubricate the thermometer with liquid paraffin or Vaseline, insert the bulb into the rectum and wait for the specified time (usually one minute). Then withdraw the thermometer, wipe it on cotton wool and examine it in a good light to read the level to which the mercury has risen. Always disinfect the thermometer before returning it to its case, using a chemical disinfectant (remember that a medical thermometer placed in boiling water will break).
Taking the pulse	The pulse can be detected by placing the hand inside the upper part of the hind leg, where the pulse can be felt in the femoral artery but it is of little value to an unqualified person in assessing the state of health.

RECOGNISING SYMPTOMS OF PAIN

Cats which are in pain tend to resent handling and the first indication that an owner may notice is when a normally friendly cat growls, or cries out on being lifted or stroked.

Strains and sprains	Muscular strains or sprains do occur in cats but they are less common than in dogs. Pain or swelling in a foot, limb, tail, or anywhere over the body surface is much more likely to be due to inflammation as a result of a small wound (usually a bite or a scratch). This usually leads to the formation of an abscess which not only causes acute local pain but may even result in a raised body temperature and general malaise (see Chapter 7).
Examination	If your cat appears to be in pain examine it carefully all over for any sign of swelling or loss of hair, which may indicate the site or cause and then of course consult a veterinary surgeon (see next chapter for advice on treatment).
	Fractures (see later under 'accidents' in this chapter)—are not always obvious or easy to diagnose. If your cat is quite unable to take any weight on a limb consult a veterinary surgeon as soon as possible.
Abdominal pain	The symptoms of abdmoninal (internal) pain are less easy to detect. However a cat which is suffering from some severe abdominal condition (such as a tumour) will generally rest in an upright position, rather than curling up comfortably and it will sometimes give a rather harsh rasping purring sound.

RESPIRATION RATE

Danger signals	The actual rate at which a cat breathes is not of much assistance to an owner in judging the state of health. However if the breathing becomes

loud, rasping or distressed this is definitely a danger signal and may indicate such conditions as pneumonia, haemorrhage in the chest following an accident, or ruptured diaphragm. The cat will as a rule sit upright and will tend to raise the head in an attempt to breathe more easily.

Distressed breathing may also be associated with catarrhal conditions but this will usually be indicated by the signs of nasal discharge.

VOMITING

Cats, like dogs, vomit very readily and this is to some extent a natural protective mechanism when they have eaten some irritant substance, or simply eaten too much.

Hair balls

Hair balls in the stomach are often expelled by vomiting and this is especially noticeable in the moulting season.

Worms

Severe infestations of round or tapeworms may cause vomiting in cats or kittens.

However if vomiting persists it is almost certainly a symptom of illness and if not checked can lead very quickly to dehydration. Consult a veterinary surgeon as soon as possible.

THIRST

As we have said before, cats do not as a rule drink very much and a sudden increase in thirst is almost always an indication of ill health. However if a cat has changed from eating canned or fresh meat to a concentrated type of semi-moist or dried food this will be likely to cause a natural compensating increase in drinking.

STRAINING

By this is meant sudden and convulsive contractions of the muscles of the abdominal wall.

Vomiting

Straining may be seen immediately before a cat vomits and it is a warning to lift it outside, or get newspapers ready as soon as possible.

Constipation or diarrhoea can produce very similar straining and it is of course important to be certain of the cause before attempting to treat the symptoms.

In the unneutered female straining may indicate the onset of birth pains.

BLADDER

Cystitis

An inflammation of the bladder may cause symptoms of straining (most often in the female). The cat will typically go to its litter tray and strain and may pass a few drops of urine or blood. However these symptoms may also indicate bladder obstruction as a result of calculi (bladder stones) in the urethra, which generally occurs in male cats. This condition is not only very painful but is extremely serious and may be fatal if help cannot be obtained quickly (see Feline Urethral Syndrome Chapter 7).

TREATMENT FOR ACCIDENTS

This of course will depend greatly on the severity of the accident and it is not always easy for an inexperienced person to assess the degree of damage. As a general guide, keep the patient quiet and warm and contact a veterinary surgeon as soon as possible to arrange for an examination and whatever treatment is needed.

Should you move the patient? As a general rule where accidents to humans are concerned the advice given is that the patient should not on any account be moved.

Where cats are concerned this advice cannot be applied in quite the same way, although it should be stressed that if any injured animal has to be moved it must be done as gently as possible, to avoid the risk of further displacement of broken bones.

If a cat is injured and lying on the road it must of course be moved to safety or there is every chance that it will be struck again by the next car.

There is also the risk that a cat lying by the road side apparently unconscious will start to come round and will then panic and bolt, only to collapse in some place where it cannot be found and helped.

Fights Unfortunately even the smallest bite or scratch from another cat is liable to result in a painful abscess (see next chapter for advice on treatment). It is not unusual to find the claw of an adversary still embedded in the wound, or in the fur of the loser.

Dogs Attacks by dogs probably occur less often than one might think, although when they do occur they are likely to be serious. Dogs will often kill young kittens, simply because it is their instinct to attack anything that runs away and if two dogs attack a cat the pack instinct to kill seems to assert itself. However if an adult cat is chased by a dog it usually makes use of its ability to climb out of danger, or if it decides to stand its ground, can often put the dog to flight.

Shock Injured animals are usually in a state of shock and the best first aid measure that can be given is to see that they are kept warm. If the cat is in a basket, cover it with a light warm blanket and place the basket near a radiator, or if this cannot be done put a well-wrapped warm hot water bottle in the basket.

Fractures It is not wise or helpful for an inexperienced person to attempt to splint a broken limb. The only practical treatment is to place the cat in a basket, or in a strong box so that it can be lifted without any unnecessary movement of the damaged leg and to contact a veterinary surgeon as soon as possible (see also Chapter 7).

Haemorrhage Superficial arterial haemorrhage is fortunately much less common in the cat than the dog. This may be to some extent because cats are more cautious and careful animals and it is very unusual for them to step on glass, or to tear themselves on barbed wire fences. In any case of severe bleeding as a result of injury to limbs, ears or tail, apply a bandage (see later in this chapter) and contact a veterinary surgeon as soon as possible. If blood continues to seep through the dressing it is best simply to apply a little more cotton wool and bandage on top of the first. To remove the dressing may only serve to disburb any clotting which has taken place.

Tourniquet This is a tight ligature which is applied above the site of injury in cases of severe arterial haemorrhage in a limb. However the risk of gangrene developing if the ligature is left in position for too long is so great that it is much safer for an inexperienced person to apply a large pressure bandage with cotton wool, as described later in this chapter.

Internal haemorrhage may often result from road accidents and is usually serious. It is recognised by extreme pallor of the gums and tongue. Keep the patient warm and contact a veterinary surgeon as soon as possible.

It is not usually wise to attempt to give a cat brandy or any other liquids by mouth when it is injured. In most cases it will cause struggling, which may be harmful and if there are internal injuries, to give anything at all by mouth is dangerous.

APPLYING BANDAGES

It must be realised that cats are not easy to bandage and the first essential is to enlist a friend to help in holding the patient. The advice given in the earlier part of the chapter on restraining a cat for examination is even more necessary when dealing with a cat which is hurt in some way.

Before commencing check that you have everything that you need within easy reach and preferably on a separate table or shelf where it will not be knocked on to the floor.

You will probably require:— any antiseptics or dressings that are to be applied, sterile gauze, cotton wool, bandages, adhesive plaster and scissors.

Fortunately cats are much less inclined to interfere with surgical wounds than dogs and it is not as a rule necessary to bandage areas where there are stitches (such as a spay wound). The exception to this is probably the Siamese as many of them will attack stitches with great determination.

Body

It is rarely possible to bandage a cat's abdomen successfully and it is probably better to construct a cotton jacket to envelop the whole of the cat's body. This need not be very complicated. A simple oblong of material with two holes for the legs to go through and a row of fastenings of some kind to secure it in place along the top of the cat's back is usually effective. For a small cat the ribbed area of a man's sock can sometimes be adapted to provide a jacket with more elasticity to keep it in place.

A body bandage suitable for abdominal wounds. If necessary two holes for the rear legs could be included.

Bandaging a foot

If this is necessary as a result of an accident, it is essential to clean the wound thoroughly to remove any dirt or grit. Bathe with a mild antiseptic solution and clip away any hair which is likely to enter the wound and prevent healing. Dust wound with an antiseptic powder, or apply whatever wound dressing has been advised by the veterinary surgeon dealing with the case and cover the wound with a piece of sterile gauze.

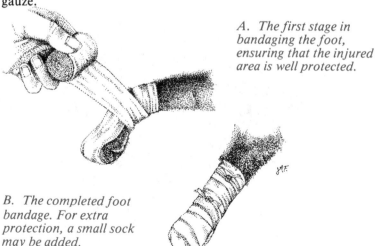

A. The first stage in bandaging the foot, ensuring that the injured area is well protected.

B. The completed foot bandage. For extra protection, a small sock may be added.

Next swathe the limb in a thin layer of cotton wool, tuck a wisp or two of cotton wool under and between the pads to prevent pressure and commence bandaging from the foot up.

Danger of gangrene—it is important to remember that wherever the wound may be on the foot or the limb, it is safer to apply the bandage over a large area and to include the foot. This allows a bandage to be applied firmly but avoids the risk of exerting too much pressure at any point in the leg. If a bandage is applied too tightly half way up a limb there is considerable risk that it will cut off the blood supply and this in turn can cause gangrene, which may be fatal.

Having applied the bandage, finish by a criss-cross application of thin adhesive plaster or Sellotape and extend this just beyond the bandage to cover a little of the fur to prevent the dressing from slipping (it can always be trimmed off with scissors when necessary to avoid the discomfort of pulling at the hair).

Bandaging an ear

Ears are often damaged when fighting and they can sometimes bleed profusely. If it is not necessary to have the ear stitched the bleeding can usually be controlled by a firm bandage.

If possible dust the wound with an antiseptic powder. Take a thick pad of cotton wool and place it over the affected ear and wrap a thin layer of wool around the head and throat. Commence bandaging (an elastic bandage is very useful here) in a criss-cross pattern around the head, pressing the injured ear flat against the head but leaving the other ear free to act as a peg to keep the bandage in place. The bandage should extend forward so as just to leave the eyes free and should continue back on to the neck. Care must be taken to see that the bandage is not applied too tightly under the throat. Finally again top the bandage with strips of Sellotape to keep it in place.

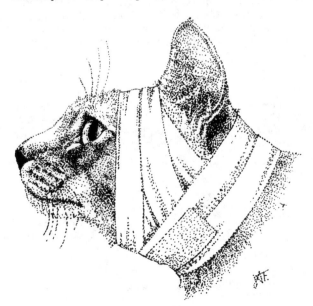

Ear bandage. The affected ear is covered, while the other is left free to act as an anchor.

Bandaging a tail
This is sometimes necessary and the same general rules apply as for bandaging a limb but it is not usually necessary to include the whole of the tail in the bandage (since there is not such a major blood supply at the tip of the tail as in the foot). However tails are particularly slippery and it may help to fold a few hairs into the bandage as it is applied to help to keep it in place. Again it is essential to finish by applying adhesive strips of some kind to cover the bandage and extend into the hair.

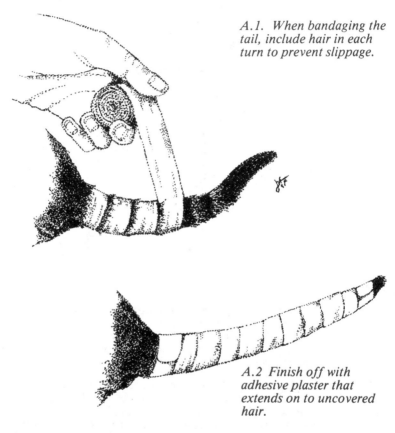

A.1. When bandaging the tail, include hair in each turn to prevent slippage.

A.2 Finish off with adhesive plaster that extends on to uncovered hair.

Abscess formation
It is important to remember that cat wounds very readily become septic, with the formation of abscesses. If you suspect that a wound is infected you should consult a veterinary surgeon. Antibiotic treatment, if it is necessary, can do a great deal to reduce the suffering resulting from this type of injury (see also Chapter 7).

Applying skin dressings
This is never very satisfactory since cats have a strong instinct to lick themselves and a dressing which was intended to be external can very easily become internal instead.

It will help if a skin dressing or other treatment is applied immediately before feeding the cat, so that it has something to distract it. However if the substance applied is in any way likely to be detrimental if taken by mouth it is better to use the Elizabethan collar.

The Elizabethan collar (so called because it resembles the type of ruff worn in the time of Queen Elizabeth I) is a very effective method of preventing a cat from biting at stitches, or from making a skin condition worse by constant licking.

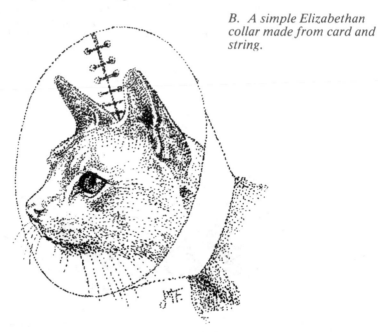

B. A simple Elizabethan collar made from card and string.

It consists of a piece of thin cardboard or really stiff paper, shaped into a funnel, rather like an icecream cone with the sharp end trimmed off. This is attached to the cat's collar with the funnel projecting forward over the head and face. Some veterinary surgeons now supply these collars ready made but they can be made quite easily at home.

It is unusual for an owner to be asked to give an injection to a cat and if it should be necessary it will be under the direct guidance of a veterinary surgeon in most instances. However in case such an emergency should occur (as for instance when living in an isolated place at home or abroad, where veterinary help may be some distance away) it may be helpful to have an idea of the method to be employed. It will also help the owner who is unused to medical procedures to understand what is involved when the veterinary surgeon may have to inject a cat.

The main methods or routes of giving an injection are as follows:-

Intravenous — In this case the injection is given directly into the blood stream, usually through a vein in the fore leg. This is often the method employed in anaesthesia.

Intra-peritoneal — The injection is given directly into the abdominal cavity.

**Intra-
muscular** — The injection is given into a muscle—usually the thick muscle of the hind leg. This route is necessary for some drugs but it is likely to cause a certain amount of pain however carefully given, as a result of the temporary pressure caused by the introduction of the liquid into the dense muscle tissue.

**Subcut-
aneous** — This is the most common route for injections and the only one in which an owner is likely to be involved. The injection is given into the space between the skin and the muscle, and causes very little discomfort or distress as a rule.

It is often given into the skin of the scruff of the neck, but in unneutered male cats this area becomes very thickened, and the skin of the hind leg may be used instead.

Hypodermic
syringes

In most cases today these are made of plastic and arrive in a sterile plastic pack, with a needle attached, which greatly simplifies the procedure of injections.

Filling the
syringe

First carefully check the amount of the dose that has to be given. Unwrap syringe from plastic cover and read off measurements on the barrel. They will be in cubic centimetres or millilitres (syringes are usually of 1, 2, or 5 cc or ml volume).

Cleanse rubber cap of bottle containing injection with a little surgical spirit.

Withdraw plunger of syringe to the amount of the correct dose, and plunge needle through centre of rubber cap.

Invert bottle and inject air into bottle (to break vacuum), then withdraw plunger until syringe contains fluid up to the appropriate mark and quickly withdraw needle from bottle.

Giving the
injection

Get an assistant to hold the patient, or if alone wrap cat up completely in a blanket, leaving out only the head and sufficient neck to inject. Part hair, and dab area to be injected with surgical spirit. Holding the skin up slightly plunge needle through skin, press plunger to expel injection and quickly withdraw the needle. Wipe over the site with cotton wool to disperse the fluid under the skin and prevent any bleeding.

All this may sound very complicated and intimidating to anyone contemplating giving an injection for the first time. However practice makes things much easier and an experienced person can give an injection so quickly and painlessly that the patient does not even bother to look round.

Enemas

An enema is a fluid preparation (usually soap and water solution) which is given by injection into the rectum, using a rubber syringe. It is used as a treatment in severe cases of constipation but it is not advisable to attempt, except under instructions from a veterinary surgeon.

If home treatment is required for cases of severe constipation (assuming that medicines taken by mouth have proved ineffective) it is safer to use a glycerine suppository. The suppository should be lubricated with liquid paraffin and inserted into the rectum where it will dissolve, producing a laxative effect (see Constipation Chapter 7).

CARING FOR THE SICK CAT

There are some conditions, in particular Cat Influenza, in which TLC as it is called today (tender loving care), can do almost as much as modern drugs in restoring a cat to health.

Cats, when they are well, keep themselves scrupulously clean by licking and grooming. In a condition such as 'flu, where there is severe nasal and ocular discharge, or if there are mouth ulcers, the cat soon becomes soiled, smelly and very wretched. A capable and devoted nurse can work wonders in restoring a cat's psychological well-being and through this, his physical welfare as well.

It is true that when a cat is very ill it should not be disturbed too much but equally it should not be neglected. The first sign of returning health in a cat is often when it starts half-heartedly at first, to wash its face and whiskers.

Keeping clean

The eyes and nose should be swabbed several times daily with cotton wool dipped in cool boiled water, to remove any discharges. This is especially necessary for the nose, to allow comfortable breathing. A cat which is forced to breathe through its mouth not only suffers distress but also further drying and soreness within the mouth as a result. The whole area of the head should then be dried with a soft flannel, or dry cotton wool. The forelegs may be soiled by the cat's attempts to rub eyes and nose. Vaseline should be applied around the nose, to prevent further drying and a suitable eye ointment used on the eyes.

If there has been diarrhoea the tail region can be cleaned in the same way and a dusting of talcum powder applied to keep the cat fresh and dry.

Force-feeding

If it is necessary to force-feed the cat it is important to repeat the cleaning-up process after each meal to prevent stale food accumulating on the hair.

Your cat will not feel like a thorough grooming but a light combing each day will help to remove dead hair and also stimulate the circulation.

Warmth

Warmth is essential in this type of illness and unless the eyes are particularly sore, the cat will probably enjoy having his basket moved into the sunshine.

Blankets and cushions are inclined to become soiled from discharges and should be changed daily.

Feeding a sick cat

Cats really hate to be force-fed, so try all possible means to tempt the appetite first. Well-stewed rabbit, hare or chicken liver are usually popular if they are available, or strong smelling fish such as kippers may be useful in cases where the cat has lost the sense of taste and smell.

Offer only small amounts of food at a time and if they are refused take them away. Stale dried-up food is unlikely to tempt a sick animal.

Dehydration (loss of body fluids) is a very serious problem, so make sure your cat's favourite drinks are always available.

It will be noticed that cats in the earlier stages of 'flu not only sneeze but sometimes literally stream at the mouth, so it is essential to see that not only milk but water is available for the sick cat at all times.

Hunger strike

After severe illnesses some cats appear to lose all interest in food and literally go on a hunger strike. In this case, if the veterinary surgeon attending the case agrees, it will probably be necessary to administer liquid foods with a spoon or an eye dropper.

For the very weak cat a mixture of eggwhite beaten and mixed with one teaspoon of glucose and one teacup of water, Lactol, or Brand's beef essence can be tried.

The most satisfactory method of administration is as described earlier in the chapter for giving liquid medicines. The amounts will vary with the cat's willingness to accept the food and swallow but it is better to be content to give only a few teaspoonsfuls at a time.

When the cat is feeling stronger and is taking food more readily then sieved meat or fish, or canned baby foods can sometimes be given quite easily with a spoon.

Chapter 7

DISEASES AND AILMENTS OF CATS

ABSCESSES

As we have said earlier (Chapter 6), cats are extremely subject to abscesses if they receive even the smallest wound and in particular as the result of bites and scratches from fellow felines, or from rats.

Symptoms of swelling and acute pain may be noticed anywhere on the body and the cat will probably be off food and listless. In the case of a bite on the foot there may be very considerable swelling giving a 'frying pan foot' appearance. If the abscess has burst there will be purulent and sometimes bloodstained discharge and the first indication may be when the cat is seen to be washing itself very vigorously.

Preventative measures—If you know that your cat has been involved in a fight examine him very carefully all over. If any bites or wounds are found clip the hair away from the area and bathe with an antiseptic lotion.

Treatment—Once an abscess has developed it is best to consult a veterinary surgeon if this is possible. Treatment with antibiotics can produce an almost instant improvement in the health and well being of the patient and will greatly speed the healing of the wound. If the abscess has developed but has not burst it may be necessary for the cat to be admitted to a veterinary hospital to have the abscess lanced and drained under anaesthesia.

First Aid Treatment—If no veterinary help is available at the time the most useful treatment is to clip away all hair from the area of the abscess and to bathe with a lukewarm antiseptic solution, several times daily.

Warning—Do not be tempted to allow an abscess to heal too quickly. If the area is not thoroughly bathed to keep the wound open until it has completely drained a new abscess will quickly form on the same site.

Tooth Abscess—See also Teeth

These occur most often in middle aged or elderly cats. The symptoms are usually refusal to eat, pain when eating, swelling on the side of the cheek, or an unpleasant smell, or a discharge from the mouth.

Treatment—Consult a veterinary surgeon as soon as possible. Even elderly cats will as a rule survive the short anaesthetic that is needed for an extraction very well (unless there is any serious heart condition), and the improvement in health will be considerable and well worth the risk. There is no need to feel concerned even if an old cat has to lose all its teeth. Most cats today take soft prepared cat foods and your pet is unlikely to have any difficulty in eating.

ANAL GLANDS

These are tiny scent glands which are situated at either side of the anus. If the cat becomes frightened it will often discharge the glands, giving a very penetrating and unpleasant smell. Anal glands in dogs are the source of many troubles and disorders but fortunately in cats it is very unusual for them to need any attention at all.

ANAL PROLAPSE—see Prolapse.

ANAEMIA

This is a symptom rather than a disease. It is characterised by a marked pallor of the gums and tongue. It may result from disease but it is most often seen when there is internal haemorrhage as a result of road accidents.

Treatment—Consult a veterinary surgeon as soon as possible and in the meantime keep the patient quiet and warm.

ARTHRITIS AND RHEUMATISM

Elderly cats may suffer from a generalised stiffness and difficulty in walking, or jumping. Since it is not at all easy for an owner to diagnose the precise cause it is best to consult a veterinary surgeon.

It will help to see that the cat sleeps in a warm dry spot.

Warning—Do not give aspirin. Although it is very helpful to humans with similar conditions, it is poisonous to cats.

ASCITES OR DROPSY

This is a condition in which fluid collects in the abdominal cavity, giving the cat a swollen pot-bellied look, although it is usually associated with generalised thinness and poor condition. It is sometimes associated with severe worm infestation, or malnutrition in young kittens but it is more often seen in older cats as a result of chronic heart trouble, or some serious internal condition such as a tumour. In either case consult a verterinary surgeon as soon as possible.

BAD BREATH

This usually results from bad teeth in the middle aged or elderly cat (see abscesses and teeth) but it may also be noticed in young kittens which are changing their deciduous teeth. Other causes may be mouth ulcers, chronic catarrh, or a tumour in the mouth, or it may result from the presence of a piece of decaying bone which has become lodged in the teeth, or from some generalised disorder such as uraemia. In any case it is a symptom which should not be ignored and which generally responds to treatment so consult a veterinary surgeon as soon as possible.

BALDNESS—ALOPECIA

It is fairly unusual for cats to suffer from a genuine baldness. If your cat develops bare places in the coat it is more often the result of skin parasites (see Chapter 5), or an eczema or dermatitis (see later in this chapter). However, Hormonal Alopecia is occasionally seen in neutered cats and this can sometimes be treated by administration, or implant of hormonal substances.

BITES—see Abscesses

BLADDER TROUBLES

These can be divided into two main divisions, cystitis or inflammation of the bladder and urethral obstruction as a result of calculi, or stones which form in the bladder. (These are actually mineral deposits which settle out to form tiny stones or gravel as they are sometimes called.)

Cystitis occurs more in female cats than males. It is characterised by symptoms of pain and the cat will be seen to go to its litter tray frequently and pass small amounts of bloodstained urine. There may also be a rise in temperature and signs of generalised illness. Consult a veterinary surgeon.

Urethral obstruction—Now commonly called F.U.S. (Feline Urinary Syndrome). This is a very serious condition requiring immediate veterinary help. It is almost unknown in female cats but occurs in male and neutered cats as a consequence of the formation of bladder stones. The urethra of the male (the passage way connecting the bladder to the penis) is extremely narrow and if tiny particles of gravel are passed in the urine they very readily cause total obstruction. In the female cat stones of similar size can be passed with the urine.

Symptoms—The cat will go to its tray and will strain hard but it will be seen that little or no urine is passed. Consult a veterinary surgeon as soon as possible. If treatment is not given at once the cat will become toxic, or may actually burst its bladder and die. In the meantime it is in great pain.

Treatment—The veterinary surgeon may be able to relieve the condition by passing a catheter tube under anaesthesia but in many cases an abdominal operation will be needed if the cat's life is to be saved. Unfortunately this condition has a tendency to recur.

Over recent years there has been a marked increase in the incidence of F.U.S. and this appears to be connected with the fact that some cats when taking a total diet of dry cat food fail to drink sufficient water to maintain a satisfactory fluid balance in the body, resulting in a rather increased concentration of mineral salts in the urine. It is seen characteristically in overweight neutered male cats which take insufficient exercise. However research work has failed to pinpoint one single causal factor for the condition and in the USA it is thought that it results from a virus infection. Fortunately at this time it appears that the increase in this condition has reached a peak and it is probably declining.

A supply of fresh drinking water should always be provided as part of a cat's normal diet but if you notice that your cat takes very little water or milk in the course of the day it is probably better to give dry biscuit only as a small part of the diet, or to use it after first moistening with warm water.

BLEEDING—haemorrhage—see Chapter 6.

BRONCHITIS

This occurs most often as a complication of cat 'flu. It is an inflammation of the bronchi and the bronchioles (the tubes connecting the lung tissue).

Symptoms—Coughing, distressed breathing—Consult a veterinary surgeon.

BRUISES

A bruise is actually made up of a mass of pinpoint haemorrhages under the surface of the skin. They do occur in animals but are often missed because of the hair (See Haematomas).

BURNS AND SCALDS

These can be a very serious problem in cats and in the case of scalds the full extent of the injuries may not be realised until several days after the event when a large suppurating area is discovered which had been hidden by the hair. Severe burns and scalds actually destroy the skin and underlying tissues and the resulting wound may take months to heal completely.

First Aid—In the case of scalds apply cold water over the affected area at once. The cat's coat will otherwise hold the hot liquid and greatly increase the extent of the injuries. Then keep the patient warm (since there will be considerable shock) and consult a veterinary surgeon as soon as possible. Remember that cats when they are frightened or in pain have a tendency to bolt, so shut all doors and windows until you are able to get help.

Prevention—Remember that cats are naturally inquisitive so try to avoid leaving them in a room where there is a saucepan of hot liquid, or any similar hazard. They should of course be trained, for their sake and yours, not to jump on to tables and work surfaces. Many cats suffer from burnt pads as a result of jumping unsuspectingly on to electric hot plates.

CAESAREAN OPERATION—See Chapter 2

This operation is carried out to remove kittens by the abdominal route in cases of difficult birth. It is as a rule a highly satisfactory method of saving the life of both mother and kittens but if it becomes necessary it is important for success that it should be carried out as soon as possible. In most cases the mother will be able to feed her kittens and they should be returned to her as soon as she starts to recover from the anaesthetic.

CANCER—see Tumours

CASTRATION

This is the name for the neutering operation in the male. See Chapter 2.

CATARACT—See Conditions of the Eye

CATARRH

This is most often seen as a complication or a result of Feline Respiratory Disease (cat 'flu), although there may be other causes.

Symptoms—Sneezing, nasal discharge, sometimes bloodstained. The cat may tend to breathe through its mouth as a result of nasal obstruction. There may be difficulty in smelling and tasting, with consequent loss of appetite and depression.

Treatment—Antibiotic treatment may give some relief but unfortunately once established this condition is extremely difficult to treat satisfactorily. Consult a veterinary surgeon.

See Chapter 6 for advice on practical measures for treatment.

CHOKING

This is fortunately less common in cats than in dogs, since cats are more careful feeders. The most common cause is a large fish bone which has become wedged in the mouth or throat.

Symptoms—Coughing, retching, attempting to vomit.

Diagnosis—To check whether your cat has an obstruction in the throat first examine mouth and throat as thoroughly as possible in a good light (see Chapter 6 on safe method of examination). If there is a visible fish bone or other obstruction it may be possible to remove it with tweezers or forceps.

If there is no visible foreign body causing the symptoms, prepare a small cube of meat or cheese (about the size of a sugar lump) and administer it as if it were a tablet. If there is any obstruction in the throat the meat will be returned at once. Consult a veterinary surgeon as soon as possible. It will probably be necessary for the cat to be anaesthetised before the obstruction can be removed.

The symptoms of convulsive coughing in the early stages of cat 'flu can easily be misinterpreted as choking.

CLAWS

These are often broken as a result of fighting. Normally they will grow again, but if the sensitive nail core is exposed the condition is very painful and may require surgery.

Infection of the nail base—In this there will be redness and swelling around the base of the nail and the cat will lick the foot constantly and show signs of lameness or pain.

First Aid—Bathe with a warm antiseptic solution but consult a veterinary surgeon as soon as possible since antibiotic treatment will probably be needed, or in some cases it may be necessary to remove the nail surgically.

CLEFT PALATE

Congenital—This is a fairly common birth abnormality. It will be noticed that the kitten has difficulty in feeding from the mother, or that milk is tending to come down its nose. On examination it will be seen that the hard palate has failed to fuse completely in the centre. The kitten will rapidly lose condition and will die. Euthanasia is recommended.

Accidental—This may be the result of a car accident, or result from a cat falling off a high balcony.

Consult a veterinary surgeon as soon as possible. It is a difficult injury but will sometimes respond to treatment.

COCCIDIOSIS

This is a disease characterised by diarrhoea (sometimes bloodstained), accompanied by loss of weight and general condition and sometimes anaemia. It is due to the presence of a protozoa (a minute parasite) in the bowel. It is relatively uncommon in cats in this country. If infection is suspected consult a veterinary surgeon.

CONJUNCTIVITIS—see Conditions of the Eye

CONSTIPATION

Constipation is not often a problem in cats. If your cat appears to be constipated and is seen to be straining do check thoroughly before attempting treatment. Similar symptoms can be shown by cats suffering from acute diarrhoea (when they may strain but only pass a few drops of fluid or blood) or by those sufering from urethral obstruction or cystitis, which is an extremely serious condition (see Bladder Troubles).

Old cats sometimes suffer from a chronic form of constipation which is probably the result of lack of exercise and loss of muscle tone in the bowel.

Treatment—Administer Sherley's Lik-A-Med Laxative or one teaspoonful of liquid paraffin daily. See Chapter 6 for best method of giving liquid medicines. If the condition does not improve consult a veterinary surgeon.

The addition of fresh liver to the diet once or twice weekly will often help to counteract a tendency to constipation.

CRYPTORCHIDISM

This is a condition in which the testicles remain in the abdominal cavity instead of descending into the scrotum (in monorchidism only one testicle is affected). See Chapter 3 page 44.

CYSTS

These are swellings on, or within the body which contain fluid.

External Cysts—Often seen around the eyes, or on the back, particularly in older cats. They are not as a rule painful or harmful and are only removed if they are in an inconvenient site, or if they are likely to be damaged.

Internal Cysts—The most common of these is the ovarian cyst, which tends to produce symptoms of continuous oestrus. Sterilisation is usually recommended.

Mammary Cysts—See also Tumours.

These are fluid-filled rather spherical swellings which occur on the mammary glands. They are more of a nuisance than a danger and should only be removed if they become damaged or if they appear to cause distress to the patient.

DEAFNESS

Congenital Deafness—This occurs in some white cats (usually those with two blue eyes). It cannot be treated and it is a considerable disadvantage since a deaf cat is very vulnerable to its enemies and is in great danger when crossing roads.

Old Age Deafness—This is probably due to fusing of the tiny bones of the middle ear and is unlikely to respond to treatment.

Deafness due to impacted wax—This is in most cases due to infection with ear mites (see Chapter 5). If in doubt as to the cause of the condition of the ear it is best to consult a veterinary surgeon.

DECLAWING—surgical

This operation is carried out under general anaesthesia and seems to cause the cat very little distress. It is usually carried out in cases where cats are particularly destructive in the house (see Chapter 4).

DERMATITIS—see Eczema and Dermatitis

DIABETES MELLITUS

This is a condition which results from the failure of the pancreas to produce insulin. It is most often seen in elderly cats.

Symptoms—Loss of weight, together with a pronounced thirst and a good appetite.

Diagnosis—By demonstrating the presence of sugar in the urine.

Treatment—Can be given satisfactorily by insulin injections, but much depends on the capacity of the individual owner to carry out the treatment which must be continued throughout the cat's life. Contact a veterinary surgeon if you suspect that your cat may be developing this condition.

DIARRHOEA

Diarrhoea is a condition in which the patient passes frequent, loose, or liquid motions. It may result from many different causes such as diet (excessive amounts of liver in the food, for instance), virus or bacterial infection, protozoa (coccidia) or bowel parasites.

Adult cat: providing the cat appears well, withhold all food and give only water to drink for 24 hours. Sherley's Anti-Diarrhoea Tablets may be given to help reduce symptoms. If this does not produce an improvement consult a veterinary surgeon.

Kittens: diarrhoea should be taken more seriously. It may result from faulty feeding, or roundworm infestation but it could be the first symptoms of Feline Virus Enteritis and in any case it may quickly cause symptoms of dehydration in the young animal. Consult a veterinary surgeon straight away.

First Aid Measures—½ teaspoonful cornflour mixed in warm water or milk and administered with a spoon or eye dropper may give temporary relief (see Chapter 6 for method of administering medicines).

DISLOCATIONS

A dislocation is the displacement of the articulation point of two bones within the joint capsule. This is comparatively uncommon in the cat.

Hip dislocation—Is occasionally seen as a result of an accident, resulting in the shortening of the affected leg.

Dislocation of the Jaw—Results in a displacement of the two jaws so that the large corner teeth are out of alignment, with inability to close the mouth. Do not attempt to correct this condition without consulting a veterinary surgeon since it may easily be confused with a broken jaw.

As a rule these conditions can be corrected by manipulation under a general anaesthetic providing that they have not been left too long.

DISTEMPER—see Cat Influenza

DROPSY—see Ascites

EAR TROUBLES—see Otitis and Haematoma

EAR MITES—see Chapter 5

ECLAMPSIA—Milk Fever

This is a condition of the mother cat while feeding her young, which results from an imbalance of calcium in the blood stream. It is much less common in cats than in dogs.

Symptoms—Muscular twitching or incoordination which may be followed by collapse and death if not treated at once. Consult a veterinary surgeon immediately.

ECZEMA AND DERMATITIS—see also Alopecia

These are the names which are usually applied to inflammations of the skin which are non-parasitic in origin. They are usually considered to be allergic in nature; that is they are the reaction of the body to some foreign substance. This may be in the food or dyestuffs in the bedding but in some cases there may be an allergic reaction to the bite of the flea, so that even the presence of one flea on the animal may set up violent itching (See also Chapter 5—External Parasites).

Symptoms—Irritation and scratching, with loss of hair. The affected cat may continuously wash and lick itself, causing serious abrasions with its rough tongue. In other words the main lesions are self-inflicted.

Miliary eczema—This is characterised by the presence of pinpoint scabs all along the back which cause extreme irritation.

Treatment—Unfortunately because the causation of these skin conditions is still not thoroughly understood diagnosis and treatment can present problems.

First Aid Measures

(1) Make sure that your cat's coat is kept clean and free from tangles and matts which set up irritation.

(2) Be quite certain that your cat is free from parasites. Many owners find it hard to accept that fleas can be found on cats in even the cleanest homes. A Sherley's flea collar if used according to the manufacturer's instructions and replaced when necessary is usually the most effective method of parasite control.

(3) Diet—check that you have not introduced any new foods into the diet which may have caused the symptoms. Try eliminating one item of food (including milk) completely from the diet for a period of two weeks at a time to see if this produces any improvement.

Local Treatment—Calamine lotion applied with a pad of cotton wool will give some local relief. However it is important to remember that any external treatment which is given to a cat is liable to become internal as a result of licking. It may help if the cat wears an Elizabethan collar for several hours after the dressing or lotion is applied (See Chapter 6).

If these simple measures produce no improvement do consult a veterinary surgeon. Modern anti-inflammatory drugs can do much to alleviate the distressing symptoms of eczema and dermatitis, but it is as well to recognise that the condition is very likely to recur.

EMPHYSEMA

This is usually seen as a complication of pneumonia. The affected portion of the lung loses its elasticity and the cat is seen to have to make a positive effort to expel the air from the chest.

ENTERITIS—non specific enteritis—see Diarrhoea

FELINE VIRUS ENTERITIS

This is a serious and often fatal virus disease which mainly affects young cats. Its incidence is greatest in pet shops, catteries, and lost cats' homes (because of the increased risk of contact with infected cats) though it may occur in private homes.

Incubation period—Symptoms are thought to develop at 4-10 days after contact with an infected cat. It is for this reason that a kitten which seemed perfectly well when it arrived in a new home can after a week become acutely ill and die.

Symptoms—Vomiting is usually the first symptom, followed by loss of appetite and diarrhoea. There may be a rise in temperature. The cat is thirsty and may often be found in the sink or in a drain. There is abdominal pain and typically the patient sits in a

hunched-up position and may even cry out. Young kittens very quickly bec
dehydrated and emaciated and for kittens of under 12 weeks the death rate is very hi

Treatment—Consult a veterinary surgeon as soon as you suspect that the disease may
be starting. There is no specific remedy for the condition but antibiotics and other
drugs will help to give some relief from the symptoms. See also Chapter 6 for advice on
general care of the sick cat.

Prevention—Vaccination may be carried out against Feline Enteritis and is highly
effective (see Chapter 3). However it must be realised that prevention will not be
effective if the cat is in the early stages of the disease.

Booster injections are needed to maintain a level of immunity (consult your own
veterinary surgeon about this) and this is particularly important if a cat has to go into
boarding kennels.

EYE CONDITIONS

Cataract—This is an opacity of the lens of the eye, which gives it a cloudy appearance
and results in partial or complete loss of vision. It is seen most in elderly cats but is not a
common condition. Surgery is possible, but is not usually recommended.

Conjunctivitis—This is an inflammation of the membrane of the eye.

Symptoms—Irritation, redness or soreness of the eye, or sometimes a discharge from
the eyes.

It may occur as an isolated condition or may be a complication of cat 'flu.

First Aid Measures—Bathe eye with cool water which has been previously boiled
but consult a veterinary surgeon for advice on further treatment.

Glaucoma—This is a condition in which there is increased pressure within the eyeball,
giving a rather swollen 'glassy' look. Most common in elderly cats, and as a
complication of cataract.

Haws (or Third Eyelid)—Cats have a third eyelid or protective membrane in the corner
of the eye. When there is any condition causing irritation of one, or both eyes the third
lid will tend to come over the eyeball and this is quite normal (although owners seeing
the condition for the first time sometimes assume that the cat is going blind).

Sometimes the condition of the third eyelid, or 'haws' as it is sometimes called, occurs
when there is no obvious local reason and it is thought that it may be a symptom of
generalised loss of condition. If it persists consult a veterinary surgeon.

Kitten's Eyes—Remember that kittens do not normally open their eyes until the 10-14
day of life.

Prolapse of the Eyeball—This is a quite common injury as a result of fighting or road
accidents. It may be possible for the eye to be returned to its socket successfully under
anaesthesia but if the eye is damaged it is better to have it removed. A cat will manage
very well with only one eye.

Staining around the eyes may result from a blocked tear duct causing an overflow of tears. Consult a veterinary surgeon.

Ulcers—Orbital ulcers are less common in cats than in dogs. They are seen as pinpoint bluish opaque areas on the eye and cause considerable discomfort. Consult a veterinary surgeon.

EUTHANASIA

If your cat has become too old to take any pleasure in life, or if it is suffering from some painful condition from which there is no prospect of permanent relief it is much kinder to ask your veterinary surgeon, or your local Animal Welfare Clinic to put your pet painlessly to sleep. This should also be considered if for personal reasons you find that you are no longer able to keep your cat. By all means try to find a new, good home for him (or her) but it need hardly be said that genuine cat lovers will never pass a pet onto just any home and will certainly not consider abandoning an animal because they are unable to face a difficult decision.

Euthanasia is now almost always performed by means of injection of a barbiturate drug, which puts the animal into a state of deep sleep which is followed by narcosis and death. The injection itself is not as a rule painful but if you dread the thought, or if your cat is very nervous ask your veterinary surgeon for a sedative tablet which you can give in advance.

The decision to have a loved pet put to sleep is always a very hard one to make but the deciding factor must always be to put the comfort and welfare of the animal concerned first, rather than any consideration of you own emotions.

FELINE RESPIRATORY VIRUS—see Influenza

FISH HOOKS

Cats sometimes become involved with fish hooks because of their liking for fish. It is important to remember that the hooks have barbs on the end and cannot be pulled out. In most cases it is necessary to consult a veterinary surgeon who will be able to remove the fish hooks quite easily and painlessly under an anaesthetic.

FITS OR CONVULSIONS

These are fortunately fairly uncommon in cats but they may be rather alarming at the time. The cat may stagger, and then rush about the room, apparently unable to see and banging into furniture and walls.

Young cats may occasionally have fits which are thought to be connected with roundworm infestation.

Older cats may have true epileptic fits (and these are likely to be repeated).

Thiamine (Vitamin B_1) deficiency has also been found to be a cause of fits.

First Aid—Do not attempt to touch the cat, but shut doors and windows and try to prevent it from harming itself too much.

Consult a veterinary surgeon as soon as possible.

FLEAS—one of the most common cat problems—See Chapter 5.

FRACTURES

Fractures are only too common as a result of road accidents. Treatment will depend on the site but an owner should never attempt to splint a leg (it could well cause more damage). Keep the patient quiet and immobilised in a basket or box and consult a veterinary surgeon as soon as possible.

Green Stick fractures may occur in young cats. The soft bones 'bend' rather than actually separate.

Fractures of limbs are now very commonly repaired by means of an internal pin, or a metal plate.

Compound Fractures—Involve an open wound at the site.

Hard Palate Fractures—See Cleft Palate.

Pelvic Fractures—Are very common. Treatment is mainly by immobilisation and recovery is dependent largely on the age of the patient and the number of pelvic bones which are affected. Healing may cause a narrowing of the pelvic canal, so it is best that female cats should be neutered as soon as possible after recovery to avoid the risk of birth complications.

Fractured Jaw—The most common site (especially in young cats) is the centre of the lower jaw. Treatment by wiring the jaw is usually very successful but it will be necessary to hand-feed the patient for the first 7-10 days (see Chapter 6 on method).

F.U.S.—FELINE URINARY SYNDROME—see 'Bladder Troubles'.

HAIR BALL

During the moulting season cats (especially long-haired cats) swallow enormous amounts of hair, and this may tend to form a hard ball in the stomach. In most cases these hair balls are vomited quite harmlessly. Obviously if you groom your cat regularly the chances of it developing a hair ball will be much less.

Cats are also inclined to chew string—especially if it has been around meat and this can cause a similar obstruction in the stomach.

Treatment—One teaspoonful liquid paraffin repeated daily may produce relief but if your cat is vomiting, or seems unwell consult a veterinary surgeon.

HAEMATOMA

This is a haemorrhage under the skin and may occur anywhere on the body as a result of a blow. It is usually seen as a darkish, not very painful swelling. It may easily be confused with an abscess, which is a much more common type of injury in the cat but in the case of a haematoma there is less pain on examination.

HAEMATOMA IN THE EAR

This is a common condition in the cat. It may result from a fight, or an accident but it most often occurs as a result of shaking the head because of the irritation caused by ear mites (see Chapter 5).

Appearance—There will be a swelling on the flap of the ear, varying from the size of a small marble to one which totally fills the ear flap.

Treatment—Consult a veterinary surgeon as an operation will be necessary to relieve the pressure and to try to keep the shape of the ear intact. If left, the ear will as a rule crumple and scar, giving the typical appearance of the 'battered' tom.

Don't forget to check for ear mites and treat these as well.

HAEMATURIA

Blood in the urine may be seen as a result of an accident causing internal bleeding or as a result of infection (see Bladder Troubles).

HAEMORRHAGE—see 'Bleeding'

HEART DISEASE

This is fortunately quite uncommon in cats. Some elderly cats may develop heart murmurs and show symptoms of lassitude and shortness of breath. Consult a veterinary surgeon if you suspect this condition.

HEAT—Oestrus or Calling—See Chapter 2

HERNIA

A hernia or rupture is the prolapse of viscera (usually abdominal contents or fat) through a gap in the muscle wall.

Umbilical and Inguinal hernia—Rarely seen but require surgical correction when they occur.

Diaphragmatic hernias—May occur as a result of an accident. In these stomach, intestines or other viscera are herniated into the chest. The cat will show distressed breathing and will be afraid to lie down. The condition is very serious so consult a veterinary surgeon.

INCONTINENCE

Lack of control over bladder or bowels is a common complication of old age in cats. Very much depends upon the individual case but the prospect is as a rule poor. Consult a veterinary surgeon.

Incontinence, or dribbling of urine in a young male cat may indicate the first signs of urethral obstruction (see Bladder Troubles and Spraying).

INFLUENZA—CAT 'FLU—FELINE RESPIRATORY VIRUS INFECTION

Cat 'flu as it is commonly called is a disease which occurs mainly in boarding kennels and cats' homes. The typical situation is that a cat either starts the disease in kennels, or symptoms develop within the first week after the return home. Owners naturally tend to blame kennel proprietors for the trouble and attribute it to neglect but this is totally unfair. No person would willingly take an infectious cat into their kennels but it seems that some cats may be carriers of the disease which they transmit to other cats without themselves showing symptoms.

The main types of the disease have now been identified as:—

(1) Feline Calici Viruses (FCV)—This is a milder form of the disease and is characterised by sneezing, discharging eyes and sometimes ulceration of the mouth.

(2) Feline Viral Rhinotracheitis—A very severe and quite often fatal type of the disease. Early symptoms are similar—typically sneezing, excessive salivation, loss of appetite and sometimes a high temperature. Later the nasal discharge becomes purulent, pneumonia may develop and the cat soon becomes dehydrated and depressed. Cases of this type which recover are liable to be left with a permanent catarrhal discharge from the eyes and nose.

Treatment—Consult a veterinary surgeon at once, but this is a situation in which good home nursing and care can also do much to help (see Chapter 6).

Prevention—A number of vaccines have been introduced against this disease recently. Some are given by injection and others by droplet inhalation and they appear to give a good level of immunity. They are certainly to be recommended and more especially if your cat may have to go into a cattery. Discuss this with your own Veterinary Surgeon.

Disinfection—Cat 'flu is spread by droplet infection, and the risk of spread is very great.

In the case of the private home it is kinder to warn other cat owners to stay away until the infection is completely cleared. In kennels disinfection is extremely difficult. Cages should be scrubbed out with a solution of washing soda in hot water and the building should be fumigated.

JAUNDICE

This is a symptom rather than a disease. Typically the tongue, gums, whites of the eyes and skin develop a yellowish tinge and the urine is dark yellow or brownish. It may be an indication of infection, poisoning, or even a tumour of the liver. Consult a veterinary surgeon at once.

KIDNEY DISEASE—NEPHRITIS

This is a fairly common disease of middle-aged to elderly cats. The symptoms are due probably to a mild and often unnoticed kidney infection early in life causing damage to the kidney structure which becomes progressively more serious. The kidneys are unable to perform their normal function of filtering impurities and waste products out of the blood.

Symptoms—Thirst, loss of appetite and loss of weight. Occasional vomiting and in the later stages an unpleasant uraemic, or ammoniacal smell to the breath.

Treatment—Consult a veterinary surgeon. While the condition cannot be cured treatment may help to alleviate the symptoms and prolong life.

LAMENESS

This is an indication of pain in a limb (or sometimes the spine). In cats the reason is much more often a septic bite than a strain or sprain.

LEPTOSPIROSIS (Leptospira canicola)

The common cause of kidney disease in dogs is extremely uncommon in cats.
Leptospira Icterohaemorrhagiae which is spread by rats and quite commonly affects dogs is almost unknown in cats.

LEUKAEMIA

This is being recognised today as a widespread disease of cats. It is a disorder of the white blood cells (leukaemic leukaemia).

Symptoms—There may be a wide variety of symptoms such as generalised loss of condition and weight, intermittent rises in temperature, thirst, anaemia and ulceration of the mouth, which make the disease rather difficult to identify.

Fortunately the most recent medical research appears to show that the disease in cats is not transmissible to humans.

LICE —see Chapter 5—External Parasites

MASTITIS

This is an inflammation of the mammary glands, seen usually in the mother cat which is feeding a litter.

Symptoms—Redness and swelling of the mammary glands, raised temperature, pain and a disinclination to let the kittens feed.

Consult a veterinary surgeon. Antibiotic treatment will as a rule produce a dramatic improvement.

MAMMARY TUMOURS —see Tumours

MANGE

Sarcoptic and Demodectic mange appear to be almost unknown in the cat.

Notoedric (head) mange is sometimes seen (see Chapter 5).

METRITIS

This is an extremely serious and often fatal condition which may follow kittening. It may occur if the cat has failed to get rid of all the kittens, or all the placentas (afterbirths), or simply as a result of infection (see Chapter 2).

Symptoms—A purulent or bloodstained discharge, rise in temperature, lassitude, loss of appetite and disinclination to care for the kittens.

Consult a veterinary surgeon at once.

MILK FEVER–see Eclampsia

This should not be confused with mastitis—the two conditions are not related in any way.

NAILS—see Claws

NYSTAGMUS

This is a condition in which the pupils of the eye move constantly from side to side. It is seen in cases of stroke, concussion and sometimes in infection of the middle ear.

OTITIS EXTERNA

A general name for conditions affecting the canal of the ear.

Bacterial Infection—Because cats have 'pricked' ears they are fairly free from bacterial infections. In the dog (or at least the long-eared varieties) the ear flap tends to create a moist atmosphere within the canal which is ideal for bacterial growth. However if your cat should show any sign of a discharge from the ear consult a veterinary surgeon.

Parasitic Otitis—This is extremely widespread among cats as a result of ear mite infection. Cats are very clean animals but the canal of the ear is one spot which they cannot reach. The condition is recognised by the presence of black wax in the ear canal. See Chapter 5—External Parasites—for details of diagnosis and treatment.

Tumours in the Ear—These are unfortunately rather common, especially in older cats. There is usually a very unpleasant-smelling discharge from the ear and the cat will scratch the ear, or keep the head on one side. Consult a veterinary surgeon. An operation may give relief, but unfortunately these tumours are sometimes malignant in nature (See Tumours).

PAINT

Cats seem to get themselves involved with wet paint quite often and the results can be very unpleasant (and this also applies to tar).

NEVER use turpentine or other paint solvents as these are poisonous to cats; not only when they are licked but because they are absorbed through the skin. Cut as much hair and paint off as possible and then rub butter or margarine into the remainder and remove with warm water and liquid detergent.

PARALYSIS

The result of damage to, or degeneration of nerves. The seriousness varies with the site.

Radial paralysis—This usually follows a blow to the shoulder damaging the radial nerve.

Symptoms—Loss of function and loss of feeling in the fore limb. The cat is unable to pick up the foot, which quickly becomes damaged and excoriated, and will become gangrenous if not treated.

Recovery is poor—if there is no improvement in 3-4 weeks, there is little chance of recovery. Amputation of the limb may be considered if the veterinary surgeon advises it. Cats and dogs manage remarkably well on three legs.

Paralysis of the tail is a very common result of injury. Again the symptoms are loss of sensation and loss of movement, and the trailing tail soon becomes damaged.

Amputation holds out a good prospect of success. A tail really is not missed at all (Manx cats manage very well without one).

PARAPLEGIA

Posterior paralysis usually results from an injury to the spine. In most cases control of bladder and bowels are lost as well as the ability to support the body on the hind limbs. If no improvement is seen within 7 days the chances of recovery are very poor indeed.

PLEURISY

This is an extremely serious condition resulting from an inflammation of the folds of tissue which separate the lungs. It may exist as a condition on its own or may follow Feline Respiratory Virus infection.

Symptoms—Very high temperature, distressed breathing, inability to lie down. The symptoms may be quite sudden in onset.

In exudative pleurisy there is free pus in the chest cavity and the condition is very rapidly fatal.

PNEUMONIA

An inflammation of the lung tissue. There is usually a raised temperature and audible and distressed breathing. It is a common complication of Feline Respiratory Virus infection. Today antibiotics can in many cases produce a rapid improvement.

POISONING

Fortunately because cats are rather careful feeders they suffer less from the results of accidental poisoning than dogs. Puppies will gobble up and swallow almost any strange thing and dogs of any age will eat dead carcasses that they find on walks but this behaviour is almost unknown in cats.

Malicious Poisoning—When people have neighbours who do not like cats there is a tendency to suspect that any illness which their pet may suffer is the result of malicious poisoning. Before jumping to conclusions it is worth considering the previous paragraph; normally well fed cats are unlikely to eat contaminated food and in addition the majority of people do not have access to dangerous poisons.

Carbolic Acid (Phenol) Poisoning—This may result from bathing cats in substances such as Lysol, since cats are very susceptible to phenol and can absorb it through the skin; any substance suspected of containing it should be avoided.

Symptoms—Twitching, convulsions followed by collapse and often death.

Turpentine poisoning—This is very similar to phenol poisoning and will often result from well-intentioned attempts to remove paint (See Paint).

'Pigeon' poisoning—In some areas the authorities use a poison to eliminate pigeons. Cats finding these dying pigeons eat them and symptoms of incoordination and narcosis are seen, which in some cases prove fatal.

Aspirin—While it is a useful drug for humans (and dogs) it can prove fatal to cats.

DDT (the insecticide) is highly fatal for cats. Always check before using an insecticide powder that it is specifically intended for cats.

What to do if you know your cat has been poisoned. If you are certain that your cat has swallowed a poisonous substance, attempt to make him vomit. The best thing to use is a small (marble size) piece of washing soda, or a strong solution of salt and water (see Chapter 6—Administration). Then contact a veterinary surgeon immediately and tell him which poison was concerned. As a general rule if no help is available remember that acid poisons should be treated by giving an alkaline solution. Bicarbonate of soda is the most likely one to be available in the home. Alkali poisons may be counteracted by giving vinegar diluted 50% with water.

In the case of external poisons (Lysol, etc) if possible remove the irritant substance by washing in warm soap and water. Keep the patient warm and contact a veterinary surgeon at once.

It need hardly be said that no sensible owner will introduce rat or mouse poisons or weedkillers into the house or garden before checking that they are safe for use with pets.

PROLAPSE

This refers as a rule to the extrusion either of the uterus (usually following kittening) or part of the bowel (usually as a result of diarrhoea). This is a serious condition and it is important to consult a veterinary surgeon as soon as possible (See Chapter 2).

Young kittens suffering from diarrhoea may suffer a slight prolapse or protrusion of the rectum and treating the cause (see Diarrhoea) will produce some improvement. However if the condition persists veterinary help should be sought.

PYOMETRA

This is a condition in which pus forms in the uterus and is comparatively uncommon in the cat. This may be to some extent because the majority of female cats are now neutered. When it exists it usually follows a history of irregular oestrus as a result of cystic ovaries.

Symptoms—A vaginal discharge, listlessness, loss of appetite, thirst. Consult a veterinary surgeon as soon as possible. Surgery is almost always necessary.

RABIES

An extremely dangerous and usually fatal disease of man and animals. It does not exist in this country because of our very strict quarantine laws. If you feel inclined to grumble at them remember how terrible the consequences would be if this disease were accidentally introduced into the British Isles (see Chapter 4).

Rabies Vaccination—This is not carried out on pets living in this country but may be necessary if you plan to take your cat abroad. Check with your own veterinary surgeon.

RANULA

A soft swelling under the tongue which may be due to a blocked or infected salivary duct. Consult a veterinary surgeon.

RICKETS

A condition of poor bone formation in the young animal resulting from an imbalance of the calcium and phosphorus ratio in the diet. It is important to remember that in the wild state cats would eat the bones of their prey thus ensuring an adequate supply of minerals. A diet which contains the correct proportion of minerals for a normal adult cat may be insufficient for the pregnant cat, or kitten.

Symptoms—Lameness, or 'knuckling' over at knee joints. Consult a veterinary surgeon.

RHEUMATISM—see Arthritis & Rheumatism

ROAD ACCIDENTS—see Chapter 6

RODENT ULCER

This actually has no connection with rats or mice at all. It was probably so-called because it occurs on the upper lip of the cat (usually near the median line), and was thought to result from catching rats.

It is a dry hard ulcerated area which is very slow to heal, although it causes little distress to the patient.

Treatment—Gentian violet was once used, but today modern drugs are more effective. Consult a veterinary surgeon.

RUBBER BANDS

Children often slip rubber bands on the legs, or round the neck of pets while playing. If not removed these may cause serious, deep wounds.

RUPTURE—see Hernia

SALIVATION

Excessive salivation is one of the first signs of Feline Respiratory Virus. It may also indicate a foreign body such as a bone stuck in the mouth, a bad tooth (see Teeth), a bee sting or maybe because your cat has licked some irritant substance. Consult a veterinary surgeon.

SCABIES —see Mange

SCALDS —see Burns and Scalds

SPAYING

This is the name for neutering in the female. See Chapter 3.

SPRAINS

Fairly uncommon in cats, since they are very skilful at landing on their feet. Occasionally strained back muscles are seen, possibly as a result of a misjudged jump.

SPRAYING

Unneutered male cats are inclined to urinate or 'spray' walls and furniture even in their own homes, especially in the breeding season. Rather inexplicably occasional cases of spraying are seen in neutered males.

STINGS

Most cats at some time attempt to catch a wasp or a bee, before learning a very painful lesson. In some cases there may be a considerable allergic reaction and the cat may salivate and be very distressed.

If it is possible to contact a veterinary surgeon the administration of an antihistamine drug will usually give immediate relief. However the symptoms will as a rule subside on their own in 1-2 hours.

TAIL INJURIES

Cats' tails, being rather exposed are very liable to injury. Treatment depends very much on the cause. See abscesses and paralysis in this chapter, and 'how to bandage a tail' in Chapter 6.

TAPEWORM —see Chapter 5—Internal Parasites

TEETH

Cats, just like people have two sets of teeth, the 'baby' or deciduous teeth and the adult permanent teeth which are cut in the period 12-24 weeks of age. Teething does not cause much trouble to young kittens as a rule but occasionally the deciduous teeth may fail to shed as the new teeth develop, giving a double set, which sometimes leads to a painful or an infected mouth.

The adult cat has a total of 30 teeth.

In the upper jaw: 6 tiny incisors at the front   lower jaw: 6 incisors
2 large canines at the corners   2 canines
6 premolars   4 premolars
2 molars   2 molars

Tartar—Many cats form heavy deposits of 'tartar' composed of mineral salts around the teeth (the deposits are often considerably larger than the teeth themselves). If this is not removed it causes soreness of the gums, bad breath, salivating and loss of appetite. It may result in gingivitis and in paradontal disease which leads to tooth decay. (Cats rarely suffer from true dental caries as do humans, probably because they take very little sugar in the diet).

Regular scaling (under anaesthesia if necessary) can do much to prevent tartar and to keep the teeth and gums healthy.

Broken teeth—The canine teeth in particular are often broken when fighting. If they are not causing pain they can be left, but infection may lead to the formation of a tooth abscess, in which case consult a veterinary surgeon. Extraction may be necessary.

Bad teeth should be removed under general anaesthetic. The gums harden and the teeth are hardly missed. See also tooth abscess under Abscess.

TEMPERATURE

For 'how to take a temperature' see Chapter 6.

THIRD EYELID—see Conditions of the Eye

THIRST—see Chapter 6.

TRAVEL SICKNESS

This is not common in cats. If a cat is a poor traveller, avoid feeding before a journey and if necessary ask the veterinary surgeon for a suitable sedative.

TONGUE

Injuries—The tongue is often injured in the course of fights and may bleed profusely. Small tears and cuts will heal on their own but if bleeding persists consult a veterinary surgeon.

Ulceration—Small smooth or pinkish areas will be seen on the tongue and there is usually excessive salivation and loss of appetite—consult a veterinary surgeon (See Ulcerative Glossitis).

TOXOPLASMOSIS

A fairly uncommon disease characterised by a high temperature and very varied symptoms. Diagnosis is not easy and depends on serological examination.

TUMOURS

A tumour is produced by the abnormal overgrowth of tissue cells. The very mention of the word is alarming to an owner but it is important to remember that tumours may be benign as well as malignant and this greatly influences the future outlook. Tumours may occur at almost any site in or on the body (even in bones) and the severity of the problem involved may depend to a large extent on their situation (for instance a tumour on the tongue or in the ear canal quickly becomes intolerable).

Benign tumours are those in which the multiplication of cells is confined to a single site and if surgically removed they will not as a rule return.

Malignant tumours (cancers) not only tend to return at the same site but are also liable to spread throughout the body by means of the lymphatic system.

Mammary tumours, so called, which are very common in female cats are sometimes simply cystic in nature but unfortunately they may also be malignant.

If you suspect that your cat is suffering from a tumour do consult a veterinary surgeon at once. You may be quite mistaken in your diagnosis, or if it is a tumour it may be 'benign'. To delay asking advice through fear may cause your pet unnecessary suffering and may lessen the chances of recovery.

ULCERATIVE GLOSSITIS

This may occur as a separate entity or may be associated with the Feline Respiratory Virus. Ulcers appear on the tongue, there is marked salivation, loss of appetite, and sometimes a rise in temperature. Consult a veterinary surgeon.

VOMITING

Vomiting in cats and dogs is extremely common and is to some extent a natural means of protection in ridding the body of noxious substances. However persistent vomiting is a danger signal and in these circumstances it is best to consult a veterinary surgeon (See also Chapter 6).

VACCINATION

Vaccination against the main virus diseases is an important step in your cat's health programme (See Chapter 3).

WORMS—see Chapter 5

WOUNDS—see Abscesses and Chapter 6.

Chapter 8
SHERLEY'S AND AMPLEX CAT CARE PRODUCTS

SHERLEY'S INTERNAL MEDICINES

Anti-Diarrhoea Tablets

Pleasantly flavoured tablets for the alleviation of symptoms in mild, uncomplicated cases of diarrhoea.

Gastrine Tablets

Formulated with antacids for the relief of indigestion, flatulence and other minor stomach disorders.

Lik-A-Med Laxative

A gentle-acting, savoury-flavoured lick-off cream laxative that is specially suitable for kittens. Given with food or placed on the nose, it is easy to administer and readily accepted.

Milk Suppression Tablets

Combined with a reduction in fluid intake, will reduce lactation. Valuable when kittens are removed from nursing mothers.

SHERLEY'S EXTERNAL MEDICINES

Canker Powder

Ideal for wet canker and otitis. Puffed into the ears it treats and soothes, killing the mange and other parasites that are a frequent cause of ear inflammations.

Canker Lotion Capsules

For dry canker and otitis. Squeeze contents of a warmed capsule into the affected ear twice a day.

AMPLEX DEODORANTS AND SHERLEY'S ACCESSORIES

Amplex Veterinary Tablets

The original Amplex tablets in veterinary form. They help to control body odours in cats.

Amplexol

A concentrated deodorant and antiseptic liquid. Used diluted, it is ideal for cleaning and disinfecting cats should this be necessary. Can also be used as a disinfectant for materials and utensils around the house.

Sherley's Breath Freshener Tablet

A specially formulated extra strength Breath Freshener Tablet for cats with breath odour. Tablets may be taken whole or crumbled and mixed with food.

Spray Away

A harmless spray for regular use around the home to neutralise animals odours on furniture and furnishings, and to deodorise kennels, cages and baskets and bedding. Pay particular attention to corners and crevices.

Stop Chew

A safe but unpleasant-tasting liquid to spray onto articles to be protected from chewing. Discourages destructive habits and can be used as often as necessary.

Swiftie

Has a special attractive odour, almost unnoticeable to humans. Used regularly on a litter tray which is each time moved nearer the door, kittens can be quickly and cleanly house trained. Helps prevent damaging accidents.

Cat Nip Mice

Delightful toy mice that all cats, young or not so young, will want to play with. Contain special herbs that are attractive to cats.

SHERLEY'S WORMING PREPARATIONS

Worming Cream

The easy-to-use worming cream for roundworm in kittens, and also adult cats to which tablets are difficult to administer. It is pleasantly flavoured and placed on the nose, around the mouth or on food, will be readily licked off.

Multi Wormer

A three week combination course of tablets that will deal with both roundworm and tapeworm at the same time. Ideal when the type of infestation is not known. Not for use in very young kittens.

Worming Syrup

Specially formulated for roundworm eradication in young kittens, in a convenient syrup presentation. Roundworm infestation, transmitted from the mother, frequently occurs in kittens and can be serious. Routine medication is advisable.

Palatable Worming Tablets

Palatable tablets specifically for roundworm. They have a pleasant savoury taste, ideal for easy administration.

Tapeworm Tablets

Specifically for tapeworm infestation, these tablets will eradicate the parasite in one day. Not for use in kittens under six months of age.

SHERLEY'S INSECTICIDES AND PARASITICIDES

Insecticidal Cat Collar

This attractive felt collar is impregnated with an insecticide that kills fleas and mites for up to 2 months. Worn continuously, it prevents further reinfestation. Adjustable and available in two sizes and four colours, it will fit all sizes of cat. It is elasticated for safety but should not be used on very small kittens.

Flea Bands for Cats

Neat plastic collars containing a strong insecticide available in two versions giving up to four months protection against fleas or up to five months protection against both fleas and ticks.

Sherley's Insecticidal Pet Powder

A normal strength insecticidal powder for use on cats, and all household pets, to control external parasites. Rapidly destroys fleas, ticks, body lice and other parasites and used regularly, will prevent further attacks. Supplied in an easy-to-use puffer-pack. Can also be used on baskets and bedding.

Sherley's Insecticidal Pump Spray

This specially designed low noise pump mechanism enables treatment of cats who are worried by the 'hissing' noise of aerosol sprays. Kills fleas, lice and mites effectively and regular treatment (including bedding and baskets) prevents reinfestation.

Sherley's Permethrin Flea Powder

Permethrin powder can be used on cats of all ages. Not only is it an efficient contact flea killer, but its residual effect gives up to 14 days extra protection against reinfestation. Should also be used on baskets and bedding.

No Scratch

Scratching is usually the first sign of fleas. Used weekly, this powder will immediately eliminate them and protect from further infection. Packed in handy puffer-pack.

SHERLEY'S VITAMINS AND TONICS

Blood Salts

Contain balanced quantities of vitamins and minerals, including vitamin A, vitamin E, copper and manganese, essential to a cat's good health. A small quantity sprinkled on the food each day will prevent any deficiency of these important nutrients.

Cod Liver Oil Capsules

A rich, natural source of vitamin A which helps to ensure a healthy coat, controls infection and maintains peak vision, and of vitamin D, which aids calcium absorption thus ensuring proper teeth and bone development.

Cooling Tablets

Cooling tablets contain a special combination of ingredients to tone and refresh the system. They can be of particular value when taken during the warmer months of the year.

Calcium Tablets

With added vitamin D to assist intestinal absorption, this important mineral is essential to the formation of strong teeth and bones. Particularly valuable for young, pregnant or lactating animals.

Lintox Tonic

Phosphate-rich, this vitamin and mineral tonic helps aid recovery after illness, builds up resistance against further disease and given daily, helps to maintain good health.

Sherley's Condition Tablets

Savoury-flavoured tablets containing a balanced combination of vitamins and minerals that all cats need to maintain top condition. A daily dose will prevent any dietary lack of these substances and help to ensure peak health.

SHERLEY'S FOODS

Lactol

Lactol is a milk food, scientifically formulated as a replacement or supplement for kittens and is also highly suitable for pregnant or nursing cats as an addition to the diet. Cow's milk is not as rich as cat's milk and is therefore not ideal for kittens. Lactol contains all the nutrients of natural cat's milk, plus added vitamins, in easily digestible form.

Lactol Drops

Milky-white chocolate drops, ideal as a treat or tit-bit for your cat. High in food energy value, they contain a balanced selection of vitamins and can be used as a supplement to the normal diet.

SHERLEY'S GROOMING AIDS

Coatacine

A non-greasy, rapid drying grooming tonic. Beautifies and imparts a rich glossy sheen to the hair. Used by breeders and exhibitors to add the final touch to an animal's appearance. Available in an easy-to-use aerosol pack.

Tear Stain Remover

A safe efficient and hygienic means of removing the unsightly stains which affect many cats' eyes. Regular use is recommended to prevent stains forming and to remove existing marks.

Index

Contents	Page No.	Contents	Page No.

Contents	Page No.	Contents	Page No.

Contents	Page No.	Contents	Page No.

Contents	Page No.	Contents	Page No.

	Contents	Page No.	Contents	Page No.

SHERLEY'S CAT CARE PRODUCTS

Sherley's Worming Preparations

Worming Cream
Multi Wormer
Worming Syrup
Palatable Worming Tablets
Tapeworm Tablets

Sherley's Insecticides and Parasiticides

Insecticidal Cat Collar
Flea Band for Cats
    (4 months protection)
Flea Band for Cats
    (5 months protection)
Insecticidal Pet Powder
Insecticidal Pump Spray
No Scratch
Permethrin Flea Powder

Sherley's Internal Medicines

Anti-Diarrhoea Tablets
Gastrine Tablets
Lik-A-Med Laxative
Milk Suppression Tablets

Sherley's Vitamins and Tonics

Blood Salts
Cod Liver Oil Capsules
Cooling Tablets
Calcium Tablets
Lintox Tonic
Sherley's Condition Tablets

Sherley's External Medicines

Canker Powder
Canker Lotion Capsules

Sherley's Foods

Lactol
Lactol Drops

Amplex Deodorants and Sherley's Accessories

Amplex Veterinary Tablets
Amplexol
Spray Away
Stop Chew
Swiftie
Cat Nip Mice

Sherley's Grooming Aids

Coatacine Aerosol
Tear Stain Remover